WALCH PUBLISHING

16 Extraordinary Hispanic Americans

Second Edition

**Nancy
Lobb**

Photo Credits

Cesar Chavez	© 1995 AP/WIDE WORLD PHOTOS
Dolores Huerta	© 2007 AP/WIDE WORLD PHOTOS
Joan Baez	© 1987 AP/WIDE WORLD PHOTOS
Ellen Ochoa	Photo courtesy of NASA
Jaime Escalente	© 1995 AP/WIDE WORLD PHOTOS
Edward James Olmos	© 1986 UPI/BETTMANN
Judy Baca	Photo courtesy of Social and Public Art Resource Center
Sandra Cisneros	© 1995 AP/WIDE WORLD PHOTOS
Roberto Clemente	© 1995 AP/WIDE WORLD PHOTOS
Henry B. Gonzalez	© 1995 AP/WIDE WORLD PHOTOS
Roberto Goizueta	© 1995 REUTERS/BETTMANN
Antonia Novello	© 1990 REUTERS/BETTMANN
José Feliciano	© 1995 UPI/BETTMANN
Ileana Ros-Lehtinen	© 1995 AP/WIDE WORLD PHOTOS
Jorge Ramos	© 2007 AP/WIDE WORLD PHOTOS
Oscar De La Hoya	© 2007 AP/WIDE WORLD PHOTOS

SGS-SFI/COC-US09/5501

2   3   4   5   6   7   8   9   10

ISBN 978-0-8251-6281-7

Copyright © 1995, 2007

J. Weston Walch, Publisher

P. O. Box 658 • Portland, Maine 04104-0658

www.walch.com

Printed in the United States of America

Contents

To the Teacher

According to *Reading Next: A Vision for Action and Research in Middle and High School Literacy*, a report to the Carnegie Corporation of New York (2004, second edition), "High-interest, low-difficulty texts play a significant role in an adolescent literacy program and are critical for fostering the reading skills of struggling readers and the engagement of all students. In addition to using appropriate grade-level textbooks that may already be available in the classroom, it is crucial to have a range of texts in the classroom that link to multiple ability levels and connect to students' background experiences."

Biographies about extraordinary people are examples of one such kind of text. The 16 Americans described in this collection should both inspire and reassure students. As students read, your instruction can include approaches that will support not only comprehension, but also learning from passages.

Reading and language arts skills not only enrich students' academic lives but also their personal lives. The *Extraordinary Americans* series was written to help students gain confidence as readers. The biographies were written to pique students' interest while engaging their understanding of vocabulary, recalling facts, identifying the main idea, drawing conclusions, and applying knowledge. The added value of reading these biographies is that students will learn about other people and, perhaps, about themselves.

Students will read stories demonstrating that great things are accomplished by everyday people who may have grown up just like them—or maybe even with greater obstacles to overcome. Students will discover that being open to new ideas, working hard, and believing in one's self make them extraordinary people, too!

Structure of the Book

The Biographies

The collection of stories can be used in many different ways. You may assign passages for independent reading or engage students in choral reading. No matter which strategies you use, each passage contains pages to guide your instruction.

At the end of each passage, you will find a series of questions. The questions are categorized, and you can assign as many as you wish. The purposes of the questions vary:

- **Remembering the Facts:** Questions in this section engage students in a direct comprehension strategy, and require them to recall and find information while keeping track of their own understanding.

- **Understanding the Story:** Questions posed in this section require a higher level of thinking. Students are asked to draw conclusions and make inferences.

- **Getting the Main Idea:** Once again, students are able to stretch their thinking. Questions in this section are fodder for dialog and discussion around the extraordinary individuals and an important point in their lives.

- **Applying What You've Learned:** Proficient readers internalize and use the knowledge that they gain after reading. The question or activity posed allows for students to connect what they have read to their own lives.

In the latter part of the book, there are additional resources to support your instruction.

Vocabulary

A list of key words is included for each biography. The lists can be used in many ways. Assign words for students to define, use them for spelling lessons, and so forth.

Answer Key

An answer key is provided. Responses will likely vary for Getting the Main Idea and Applying What You've Learned questions.

Additional Activities

Extend and enhance students' learning! These suggestions include conducting research, creating visual art, exploring cross-curricular activities, and more.

References

Learn more about each extraordinary person or assign students to discover more on their own. Start with the sources provided.

To the Student

The lives of many Hispanic Americans have made a difference in the story of America. Writers, artists, scientists, teachers, politicians, ministers, lawyers, doctors, businesspeople, athletes, and so many more have helped to make America what it is today. Hispanic Americans can be proud of their heritage. And it is a pride all Americans should share.

In this book you will read the stories of:

- Cesar Chavez, who used nonviolent tactics to gain better wages and working conditions for farm workers

- Dolores Huerta, who co-founded the United Farm Workers with Cesar Chavez

- Joan Baez, the internationally famous folk singer who has worked for antiwar and civil rights causes

- Ellen Ochoa, an astronaut who soared into outer space on the space shuttle Discovery

- Jaime Escalente, whose tough teaching methods and belief in his students inspired them to excel in mathematics

- Edward James Olmos, an award-winning actor who speaks out against violence and promotes education

- Judy Baca, an artist who planned and helped young people paint the largest outdoor mural in the world

- Sandra Cisneros, a well-known author who tells the stories of strong Hispanic women

- Roberto Clemente, the first Hispanic American to enter the Baseball Hall of Fame

- Henry B. Gonzalez, who served the American people with honesty and independence for 38 years in the U.S. Congress

- Roberto Goizueta, who, as chairman of the Coca-Cola Company, was in the top ranks of American business

- Antonia Novello, the first woman and the first Hispanic American to serve as surgeon general of the United States

- José Feliciano, who, despite blindness and poverty, became an internationally known singer and guitarist

- Jorge Ramos, one of broadcast journalism's most influential news anchors

- Ileana Ros-Lehtinen, the first Hispanic-American woman to be elected to the United States Congress

- Oscar De La Hoya, a boxing champion who has given back to his community

The motto on the Great Seal of the United States reads *E Pluribus Unum.* That is Latin for "Out of many, one." The United States is made up of many people from many races. These people have come together to form one nation. Each group has been an important part of American history. I hope you will enjoy reading about 16 Hispanic Americans who have made a difference.

—Nancy Lobb

Background Information

Who are the Hispanic Americans?

The U.S. government defines "Hispanics" as people who speak Spanish or who are of Spanish, Portuguese, or Latin-American (Central or South American) descent. The three largest groups in the United States are Mexican Americans, Puerto Ricans, and Cuban Americans.

Just as there is a wide variety of Hispanic groups, there are many different terms these groups use to refer to themselves. The term *Hispanic* is a general term that includes all of these groups.

Some prefer the term *Latino* instead of Hispanic. Other Hispanic Americans refer to themselves based on their heritage—that is, Cuban American, Mexican American, Puerto Rican, and so forth. Some Mexican Americans prefer the term *Chicano.*

In this book, we have chosen to use the broader term *Hispanic American* to refer to all those with Spanish ancestry.

How many Americans are Hispanic?

A 2005 census update showed there were 41.8 million Hispanic Americans in the United States. (That is 14 percent of the country's total population of 290 million.)

The Hispanic population is increasing quickly. Half of the population increase is due to immigration, mostly from Mexico. A second reason is the high birthrate among Hispanics.

Where do Hispanic Americans live?

Most Mexican Americans live in Texas, New Mexico, Colorado, Arizona, and California. Puerto Ricans live mostly in New York, New Jersey, and Illinois. Most Cuban Americans live in Florida.

In 2005, almost two thirds of Hispanic Americans lived in 25 large U.S. cities. In Los Angeles County, there are 4.6 million Hispanic Americans. That makes Los Angeles the second largest Spanish-speaking city in the world! (Mexico City is the largest.)

Why are so many countries Spanish-speaking?

At one time, Spain was a world superpower. Spaniards put much energy into exploring and conquering new parts of the world. They settled much of North and South America. In 1492, Columbus landed in America. The first Spanish settlement in North America was at St. Augustine, Florida in 1563.

In Mexico, the Spanish conquered the native Indians. Intermarriage over the years produced the Mexican people (*mestizo*). Thus, the heritage of Mexicans is both Indian and Spanish.

Cuba and Puerto Rico were conquered by the Spanish, as well. The Spanish forced the native Indians into slavery. They also imported many African slaves. Thus, Cubans and Puerto Ricans have a Spanish, Indian, and African heritage.

Why did Mexicans immigrate to the United States?

Many Mexicans became U.S. citizens in the 1800s. In 1821, Mexico declared its independence from Spain. Then in 1848, Mexico lost the Mexican War to the United States. The Mexicans had to give up the northern half of their land, including what is now California, Arizona, Utah, and Nevada, to the United States.

At that time, Mexicans living there were given the choice of becoming U.S. citizens or returning to Mexico. Eighty percent stayed and became U.S. citizens. Later, additional territory was purchased from Mexico. This land became part of Arizona and New Mexico. Many Mexican residents in this area became U.S. citizens.

In the late 1800s, more Mexicans came to the United States seeking jobs as the Mexican economy weakened. They worked as farm and ranch hands, railroad workers, miners, and factory workers.

Today, thousands of Mexicans continue to migrate north each year seeking work. There are always many Mexican immigrants, both legal and illegal. In 2005, there were 26.8 million Mexican Americans in the United States.

Why did Cubans immigrate to the United States?

Before 1959, there were few Cuban immigrants. But in 1959, Fidel Castro overthrew the Cuban government and declared Cuba a communist state. He outlawed individual ownership of property and accumulation of wealth. Many middle- and upper-class Cubans fled Cuba. Castro allowed them to take only the clothes on their backs and five dollars in American money. The Cuban government took the rest of their wealth. Most of these people ended up in Miami, Florida. Most of them were educated, professional people who were welcomed into the United States.

A second large group of Cubans was allowed to leave Cuba in 1980. This "boat-lift" of Cubans was controversial because, unlike the first group, most of these people were from the lower class. A number were even criminals or mentally ill individuals who Castro wanted to get rid of.

The number of Cubans in the United States rose from 30,000 in 1959 to 1.4 million in 2005. Cubans are a major force in Florida, especially in Miami.

Why did Puerto Ricans come to the United States?

In 1898, following the Spanish-American War, Puerto Rico became a territory of the United States, and in 1917, Puerto Ricans were granted U.S. citizenship. Since that time, Puerto Ricans have had the right to travel unrestricted between the island and the mainland.

After World War II, the economy of Puerto Rico began to weaken. Many Puerto Ricans have come to the United States since then. In 2005, there were approximately 3.8 million Puerto Ricans living in the United States. Most of these people live in New York City. About 3.8 million Puerto Ricans still live on the island of Puerto Rico.

What other countries do Hispanics come from?

Immigrants come from Latin American countries such as Nicaragua, Guatemala, Honduras, Colombia, the Dominican Republic, and El Salvador. Most come to escape civil war, poverty, and political repression.

The 1969 border war between Honduras and El Salvador caused economic conditions to deteriorate in all of Central America. Civil wars and unrest in Guatemala, El Salvador, and Nicaragua since 1979 have caused large migrations. The number of Central and South Americans in the United States was about 5.2 million in 2005.

Cesar Chavez

Civil Rights Champion

Cesar Chavez was a civil rights leader. He led *La Causa*, migrant workers' fight for their rights. Chavez won great gains for these workers. He has been called the Mexican-American Dr. Martin Luther King Jr.

Cesar Chavez was born in 1927 near Yuma, Arizona. In 1938, his family lost their farm because they could not pay their taxes. With many others, they left for California where they had heard there was work.

The Chavez family became migrant workers. This meant they traveled from farm to farm picking crops. They lived in labor camps. Home might be a tent. It might be a one-room shack. There would be no running water and no bathroom.

The life of the migrant workers was hard. Most of the work was "stoop labor." That meant the pickers had to bend over all day to pick the crops. They also had to stoop to hoe weeds using a short hoe. For this backbreaking work, they were paid very little.

Some farmers even cheated the workers out of the little they earned. The workers could not speak English. They feared being sent back to Mexico. So there was little they could do to fight back. Life in Mexico was even harder.

The Chavez children went to school when they could. Cesar later said he went to over 65 grade schools "for a day, a week, or a few months." Cesar finished eighth grade. This was far more education than most migrant children got.

But Cesar also taught himself. He was always reading. He loved the works of Mahatma Gandhi and Dr. Martin Luther King Jr. From these men, he learned the idea of nonviolent protest.

During World War II, Cesar served in the Navy. When he returned, he married his girlfriend, Helen. They began working on a farm near San Jose with seven other family members. Later, Cesar figured out that the nine workers put together were making 23 cents an hour!

Cesar joined the Community Service Organization (CSO). This group was working to help Mexican Americans better themselves.

Cesar worked in the fields by day. At night he worked to get Mexican Americans to register to vote. In just two months, he signed up 4,000 workers.

The farm owners found out what Cesar was doing. They were afraid he would make trouble. So they fired him. Cesar began working full time for the CSO. He held meetings to get more workers to join the CSO.

Cesar worked ten years for the CSO. Then in 1962, he left the group. He wanted to form a farm workers union. The CSO did not. So Cesar went out on his own.

Chavez, his wife, and eight children moved to Delano, California. Using their life savings of $1,200, they formed the National Farm Workers Association (NFWA) with the help of Dolores Huerta. This group later became the United Farm Workers (UFW).

Workers were glad to sign up. Their motto was the phrase *¡Sí, se puede!* ("Yes, it can be done!") The union would become Chavez's life work.

Three years later, the NFWA gained worldwide attention. It joined a strike, or *huelga*, against grape growers in the Delano area. It was this *huelga* that brought fame to Cesar Chavez.

It all began when Filipino grape pickers went on strike for higher wages. The NFWA joined in. The strike was to go on for five years.

The story of Cesar Chavez and the migrant workers soon spread all over America. Newspapers and TV spread the story of *La Causa*. In 1966, 10,000 people from all over the United States marched from Delano to Sacramento. Still, the grape growers would not give in.

Cesar knew the public supported the farm workers. So he announced a boycott of California grapes. This meant that no one would buy grapes unless farmers met some of the workers' demands.

Cesar sent workers to different cities all around the United States. They asked store owners not to sell grapes. They asked the public not to buy grapes. Many truck drivers agreed not to haul grapes. The boycott spread. Many grape growers went out of business. The strike went on.

After a few years, some of the strikers began to get tired. They wanted to use more violent methods of getting what they wanted. Riots, dynamite, and shooting were suggested. But Cesar insisted on using only nonviolent tactics. So he began a 25-day hunger strike.

Cesar Chavez won the support of civil rights groups and churches. Many famous Americans joined *La Causa*. Robert Kennedy was a close friend of Chavez. Dr. Martin Luther King Jr. supported Chavez. Union leaders and even the pope supported *La Causa*. Money to help the striking workers came, too. At last, the grape growers gave in. After five years, the grape boycott was over. So was the strike. Cesar and the farm workers had won.

Over the next 20 years, Cesar kept working to help the farm workers. He demanded an end to the use of dangerous pesticides on crops. He won rest periods for pickers. And the hated short hoe was banned.

In the 1970s, Cesar led a lettuce boycott and another grape boycott. In a 1972 protest over right-to-work laws, he went on a 24-day fast. In 1988, he went on a 36-day fast to protest the use of pesticides in fields. This damaged his kidneys.

In 1993, Cesar died at the age of 66. Doctors said his death was caused by fasting and a life of hardship.

Cesar Chavez had devoted his life to *La Causa*. All his life he chose to live penniless. He never owned a house or a car. He never earned more than $6,000 in his life. The rest of the money he raised was poured back into the UFW. Although his health was failing in his later years, he never quit working for the union.

In 2006, the California Hall of Fame was created. Its purpose is to honor great Californians. One of the very first people to be inducted into the Hall of Fame was Cesar Chavez.

Cesar Chavez was one of the truly heroic figures of the 20th century. He gave dignity and hope not only to farm workers, but to all Mexican Americans. Cesar Chavez was a giant in the civil rights movement of the United States.

Today, new leaders are needed to speak up for migrant workers. Almost half of all farm workers today are in the United States illegally. Many farm workers are making the same wages that were paid 25 years ago. It will be a hard task for anyone to fill the shoes of Cesar Chavez.

Remembering the Facts

1. Why did the Chavez family lose their farm?

2. What is "stoop labor"?

3. Why didn't the migrant workers fight back when they were poorly treated by large growers?

4. How did Cesar Chavez educate himself?

5. What was the purpose of the Community Service Organization?

6. Where did Cesar get the money to form the National Farm Workers Association?

7. What were some of the nonviolent tactics that Cesar used?

Understanding the Story

8. Cesar Chavez used only nonviolent protest. If he had allowed his union members to use violence, what do you think might have happened?

9. Cesar Chavez was fighting for the farm workers at the same time Dr. Martin Luther King Jr. was fighting for civil rights for African Americans. In what ways are their lives alike?

10. Why do you think Cesar Chavez chose to live his life penniless?

Getting the Main Idea

Why do you think Cesar Chavez is a good role model for the youth of today?

Applying What You've Learned

Imagine that you are a Mexican-American teenager living in California in the 1950s. Your family all work as migrant farm workers. Describe a day in your life.

Dolores Huerta

Civil Rights Activist

Lettuce and tomatoes. Spinach, broccoli, and cucumbers. Strawberries and peaches. All of these crops and many others must be picked by hand. Growers need lots of workers to do this hard work. Most of the people willing to do this work are migrant workers from Mexico. They are called migrants because they migrate from one area to another as the crops are ready to be picked.

Most of these workers are poor. They have little education. Many do not speak English. And many are in the U.S. illegally. Because of these facts, it is easy to treat the workers unfairly.

For many years, the United Farm Workers (UFW) has helped farm workers organize to improve their lives. Delores Huerta and Cesar Chavez co-founded the UFW in 1962.

Among Mexican Americans, Huerta is a folk hero. She is shown on murals. She is celebrated in songs. Today, she continues to work for the rights of farm workers.

Dolores Huerta was born Dolores Fernandez on April 10, 1930 in Dawson, New Mexico. Her parents divorced when she was five. Her mother moved Dolores and her brothers to Stockton, California, to live with her grandfather.

Dolores' mother was a model of strength, independence, and ambition. She worked hard to support her family. She was a waitress and a cook during the day. At night, she worked in a cannery. She managed to save enough money to buy two small hotels and a restaurant.

Dolores and her siblings lived in one of the hotels. They all helped with the daily cleaning and renting of the rooms. Dolores' mother often put up farm workers and their families for free.

Although her father lived in New Mexico, he also inspired her. He was active in labor unions. Later, he went back to school and earned a degree. In 1938, he won election to the New Mexico state legislature. There he worked for better labor laws.

Dolores took free dance lessons that were offered in Stockton. She grew up thinking she would be a dancer. She was also active in the Girl Scouts until she was 18. Her troop was active in many community service projects. She won second place in a national Girl Scout essay contest.

Dolores was an excellent student. In English her senior year, she received *A*'s on all her work. However, she was given a *C* on her report card. The teacher did not believe Dolores could have written the stories herself (because she was Hispanic).

Dolores earned a teaching degree from Stockton College. She got a job as an elementary school teacher. Most of her students were the children of farm workers. They came to school in old clothes that did not fit. They did not have enough to eat. And they missed a lot of school because they had to help in the fields.

Dolores was soon frustrated. She felt she was unable to meet her students' many needs. She later said, "I couldn't stand seeing kids come to class hungry and needing shoes. I thought I could do more by organizing farm workers than by trying to teach their hungry children."

In 1955, Dolores met Fred Ross. Ross was an organizer working for the Community Service Organization (CSO). He had come to Stockton to organize a local chapter of the CSO. Dolores was hired by the CSO. She registered people to vote. She organized citizenship classes for immigrants. And she tried to get the city to improve Hispanic neighborhoods.

Because of her skill, the CSO sent Dolores to the state capital in Sacramento as a lobbyist. She was a 25-year-old Hispanic woman. In the mid-1950s, neither women nor minorities were respected in the capitol. But Dolores soon gained the legislators' respect.

It was in the CSO that she met Cesar Chavez. Both Cesar and Dolores wanted to start a union for farm workers through the CSO. But the CSO was not interested. So the two left the CSO. In 1962, they co-founded the National Farm Workers Association (NFWA).

Dolores later said, "People thought we were crazy. They asked, 'How are you going to organize farm workers? They are poor, powerless immigrants. They don't have any money and they can't vote.'"

It was the strike against California grape growers that made Cesar Chavez, Dolores Huerta, and the NFWA famous. The strike began with the grape growers union. The NFWA supported the strike. In 1966, the two unions merged. The United Farm Workers Organizing Committee (UFWOC) was formed. After 1972, this union was known as the UFW.

Dolores was the UFWOC's chief negotiator. By 1967, she had won gains for the workers with some wine-grape growers. She negotiated an agreement that raised the farm workers' wages. She also won the first medical and pension benefits for farm workers in history.

However, most of the table grape growers would not give in. So, in 1968, the UFWOC called for a national boycott of California table grapes. Dolores went to New York City to direct the boycott there. People all across the United States refused to buy grapes. Finally, in 1970, the growers gave in. Dolores negotiated new contracts with the growers. She won many benefits for the grape pickers.

The strike had made it clear that there were ties between the farm workers' struggle and the civil rights movement in the South. In 1966,

Dr. Martin Luther King Jr. sent a telegram to the UFW. He said, "The fight for equality must be fought on many fronts—in the urban slums, in the sweat shops of factories and fields. Our separate struggles are really one—a struggle for freedom, for dignity, and for humanity. We are with you in spirit."

In 1975, the California state legislature passed the Agricultural Labor Relations Act (ALRA). Dolores had lobbied long and hard for it. The ALRA was the first law of its kind in the United States. It guaranteed the right of farm workers to form a union. It required growers to negotiate with the union. This law was a triumph for the UFW.

Dolores and Cesar Chavez were alarmed about the effects of pesticides on farm workers. Pesticides caused illness and death. They also caused birth defects among the workers' children. In 1984, the UFW made a list of the most dangerous pesticides. Because of their work, many of these were banned.

In 1985, Dolores lobbied for a law to help farm workers who had lived, worked, and paid taxes in the United States for many years. These workers had not been able to become citizens. Dolores's work resulted in the Immigration Act of 1985. This law gave 1,400,000 farm workers amnesty.

Dolores worked with Cesar Chavez for over 30 years. They founded the first medical and pension plans for farm workers. They founded the Farm Workers Credit Union. They formed the National Farm Workers Service Center, which provides affordable housing. They even started nine Spanish-speaking radio stations.

After Cesar Chavez's death in 1993, Dolores continued the fight. She organized strikes. She directed boycotts. She negotiated contracts and worked as a lobbyist. She was arrested dozens of times for union activities.

Sometimes her activities put her in danger. In 1988, George H.W. Bush was running for president. He was speaking at a fundraiser in San Francisco. Republicans were not usually supportive of the farm workers. So Dolores organized a peaceful protest outside the hotel where he was speaking.

A police officer asked the protesters to move back from the entrance. Dolores and the others did. But one officer knocked Dolores to the ground with his baton (club). She had several broken ribs and a ruptured spleen.

The attack was recorded on video. Dolores sued the city of San Francisco. She was awarded an $825,000 settlement. She used most of the money from the settlement to form the Dolores Huerta Foundation. This group works to organize poor and working communities to get gains in housing, health, and jobs.

Dolores married Cesar Chavez's younger brother Richard. The couple had four children. Dolores had seven other children from earlier marriages. She was now raising eleven children. Today, her children credit her with giving them a sense of civic duty. She also inspired them to work hard and succeed in their careers.

In 1992, Dolores led a 165-mile march from Delano to Sacramento, California. She wanted the governor to sign a bill that required mediation in cases of disagreements between farm workers and growers. She was 72 years old at the time. The governor gave in and signed the bill.

In 1992, she was the second person to win the Puffin Prize by the Nation Institute. The award is given yearly to a person who has given a lifetime of sacrifice for a cause. Dolores used the prize money to form an institute to train new organizers for the future. It is called the Dolores Huerta Foundation's Organizing Institute.

Dolores Huerta has won many awards. In 1993, she was inducted into the National Women's Hall of Fame. In 1998, she was named one of the "100 Most Important Women of the 20th Century" by *Ladies Home Journal*. President Clinton awarded her the Eleanor Roosevelt Human Rights Award in 1998. In 2000, she won the Hispanic Heritage Award. In May 2006, Dolores was awarded an honorary degree from Princeton University.

In 2003, Dolores resigned from the UFW. She still works long hours as President of the Dolores Huerta Foundation. She speaks across the nation on issues that affect immigrants, women, and children. There is still much work to be done. She has stated, "Immigrants are the new civil rights movement. They need to know how they can participate in the political process."

In 2003, Dolores spoke at the Dolores Huerta Elementary School in Stockton. Most of the students there are children of farm workers. She told the students, "Your parents and grandparents do the most sacred work in the world. They feed everybody."

Remembering the Facts

1. How was Dolores's mother an inspiration to her?

2. How was Dolores's father an inspiration to her?

3. Why did Dolores give up her work as a teacher?

4. What made the NFWA famous?

5. Why was the ALRA important?

6. Why were Dolores Huerta and Cesar Chavez concerned about pesticides?

7. What is the purpose of the Dolores Huerta Foundation?

Understanding the Story

8. Why do you think Dolores was named one of the 100 Most Important Women of the 20th century?

9.   Why do you think Dr. Martin Luther King Jr. told Huerta, "Our separate struggles are really one"?

10.   Why do you think Dolores says that immigrants are the new civil rights movement?

Getting the Main Idea

Why do you think Dolores Huerta is a good role model for the youth of today?

Applying What You've Learned

Dolores says that the goal of her foundation is to "show people how to work together and take on the issues that are affecting them." Choose an issue that affects students in your school. Make a list of ways Dolores might advise students to get this issue addressed.

Joan Baez

Singer and Activist

Joan Baez was born in New York in 1941. Her father taught physics. His family had come to the United States from Mexico when he was a baby. Baez's mother was from Scotland.

The Baez family were Quakers. The Quaker religion teaches nonviolence. This idea would become the guiding force of Joan's life and her music.

As a child, Joan struggled in school. Many years later she learned that she was dyslexic. This made reading hard for her.

But Joan was talented in art and music. In high school, she began singing and playing the guitar for groups of friends. Soon she was asked to play for groups around her area.

The Baez family moved to Boston. Folk music was popular in that area. Soon Joan became part of the folk music scene.

Folk songs fit the mood of the young people of America in the 1950s and early 1960s. It was a time of protest, marches, and boycotts. The civil rights movement was growing. Joan Baez became the best known of the folk singers.

In 1959, Joan made her professional debut. The 18-year-old amazed 13,000 people at the Newport Jazz Festival. Her hair was long and straight. She was barefoot. Her beautiful voice soared over three full octaves to thrill the crowd. She leaped to instant stardom.

Joan signed a contract with Vanguard, a small folk music label. Her first record album, *Joan Baez*, came out in 1960.

In 1962, *Time* magazine did a cover story on Joan. The story said that, "her voice is as clear as air in the autumn, a vibrant, strong, untrained, and thrilling soprano." It went on to dub Joan Baez the Queen of Folk Music.

Joan sang songs that were very, very old. But she was in tune with the problems of her day. In 1962, she got involved in the civil rights movement. On tour in the South, she performed only at black colleges. She did this to protest discrimination against blacks. She later took part in marches with Dr. Martin Luther King Jr.

In 1963, Joan met Bob Dylan. Dylan was then an unknown songwriter. Dylan and Baez began to do concerts together. They became known as the King and Queen of Folk Music.

Hidden in the old songs Joan sang were messages about social issues. She sang about the underdogs of society. She sang of inequality of the races. She sang about poverty. She sang of the uselessness of war. Finally, she sang of redemption and grace.

True to her Quaker roots, Joan has always stood for nonviolence. From 1964 on, she did not pay 60% of her income taxes. She figured this amount would have been spent on building weapons. She wrote a letter to the U.S. government explaining her decision. It was printed around the world. (The IRS got its money. It was collected from the cash register at her performances.)

Joan went to jail twice in 1967 for anti-Vietnam War protests. Her version of the song "We Shall Overcome" became the anthem of the civil rights and antiwar movements.

Joan was involved in other causes, too. She supported Cesar Chavez and *La Causa*. She worked against capital punishment. She worked for the draft resistance movement. She co-founded the Institute for the Study of Nonviolence and Amnesty International.

In 1968, Joan married David Harris. He was later jailed for three years for refusing to be drafted. They had one son. The marriage lasted only three years.

With the end of the Vietnam War, Joan began singing about injustice in other countries. She dedicated an album to those living under the rule of a dictator in Chile. This album was sung entirely in Spanish. One of the songs on this album was "We Shall Not Be Moved." This song had been banned in Spain for the previous 40 years.

In the mid-1970s, Joan started writing many of her own songs. The best known song she has written is "Diamonds and Rust."

Meanwhile, Joan continued to work for causes she believed in. In 1972, she traveled to North Vietnam with a peace group. She talked about human rights in the area. She also delivered gifts to American prisoners of war.

Joan helped start a U.S. branch of Amnesty International. This group works to improve human rights around the world. Next, she started her own human rights group, Humanitas International.

She toured Chile, Brazil, and Argentina in 1981. But she was not allowed to perform in these countries. The dictators there were afraid she would reach too many people with her human rights message.

Joan continued her political activities in the 1980s. She sang at rallies for the nuclear freeze movement. She traveled to Ireland, calling for an end to violence there.

Joan has performed at countless benefit concerts. In 1985, she performed at the Live Aid Concert to fight hunger in Africa. In 1986, she sang for Amnesty International's Conspiracy of Hope tour. Also in 1986, she performed at The People's Summit Concert in Iceland. In 1988, she sang for a benefit for Amnesty International.

In 1993, Joan was asked to perform in the war-torn cities of Sarajevo and Zagreb in the former Yugoslavia. She was in the middle of a tour at the time. But she canceled her performances and went to Sarajevo. She said, "In a situation like this (wartime), the only thing that gives people any hope, any beauty, anything to refresh the soul is the arts."

In the 1980s, Joan's music career began to decline. Sales of her records were down. Folk music was out of style. This was a hard time for Joan Baez. But she was determined to keep singing. She changed her style to a kind of folk-rock. She began writing her own songs. She also sang tunes from other, younger writers. Her 1992 album *Play Me Backwards* was considered one of her best albums in years.

In 2001, Vanguard Records began re-issuing a series of Joan's albums on CD. The series included every one of the 13 original albums she recorded between 1960 and 1972. This was the largest re-issuing program ever focused on one artist!

Joan has received many awards in her career—some for music, and some for her human rights work. In 2000, she received a lifetime achievement award. To date, she has recorded nearly 60 albums. Eight of these became a gold record.

In 2003, Joan performed at two rallies protesting the U.S. invasion of Iraq. In 2004, she toured college campuses. She urged students to vote for peace candidates. In 2005, she sang at an anti-war protest at the Texas ranch of President Bush. Later that year, she performed at an anti-war rally in Washington, DC.

Joan Baez's art is a tribute to the power of music. Her songs have healed and inspired Americans for decades. Almost 50 years after she recorded her first album, she has never been more loved by her fans.

Remembering the Facts

1. What teaching of the Quaker religion was the guiding principle of Joan Baez's life?

2. Why did Joan Baez do poorly in school?

3. What kind of music did Joan sing in the early 1960s?

4. When and where did Joan gain instant stardom?

5. Name two causes supported by Joan in the 1960s.

6. What is the goal of Amnesty International?

7. Name a benefit concert performed by Joan.

8. What did Joan protest between the years 2003 and 2005?

Understanding the Story

9. What do you think is the significance of Vanguard Records' re-issuing of Joan's 13 original records?

10. Joan Baez did a concert in Sarajevo in 1993. The city had been under siege for a year. After the concert, one person told her, "Thank you for coming here. You've brought us life." Why do you think the person said that?

Getting the Main Idea

Why do you think Joan Baez is a good role model for the youth of today?

Applying What You've Learned

How do you think Joan Baez's music has influenced young people in positive way?

Ellen Ochoa

Astronaut

September 12, 1993 was a beautiful day at Cape Canaveral, Florida. The space shuttle *Discovery*'s engines roared to life. Its mission in space was about to begin.

On board *Discovery* were five astronauts. One of them was Dr. Ellen Ochoa. She was the first female Hispanic astronaut.

Ellen was born in 1958 in Los Angeles, California. She grew up in La Mesa, California, with three brothers and a sister. Ellen's father worked for Sears. Her mother stayed home to raise their five children.

When Ellen was in middle school, her parents divorced. She credits her mother with her success. Ellen's mother told her children they could succeed at whatever they wanted to do. She stressed the value of going to college. All the Ochoa children worked hard and did well in school.

Ellen was a good student. She loved math and science. But she did well in all her courses. She graduated from high school first in her class.

Ellen also became an excellent flute player. She won many awards for her playing.

Ellen won a scholarship to Stanford. But she turned it down. She needed to stay closer to home. Her mother needed help with her younger brothers.

So Ellen went to San Diego State University instead. There she earned a degree in physics in 1980. Again she graduated first in her class.

Ellen went on to Stanford. She earned a Ph.D. in electrical engineering in 1985. During all her years in school, she earned straight *A*'s. She was a hard worker and a brilliant student. While at Stanford, Ellen was also a soloist with the Stanford Symphony Orchestra.

From 1985 to 1988, Ellen worked as a researcher. During this time she received three patents in optical processing.

In 1988, Ellen got her pilot's license for small planes. She was thinking about becoming an astronaut. She knew it would be a good idea to learn about flying.

Ellen first applied to become an astronaut in 1985. She was turned down. But she didn't give up. She applied again in 1987. This time she was accepted as one of 100 finalists.

In 1988, she began working for NASA as a researcher. She moved up the ladder quickly. Soon she was supervising 35 other scientists.

In 1990, Ellen married Coe Miles. He was also a research engineer. They later had one son.

Ellen began training to be an astronaut in 1990. There was a lot to learn. The training was tough and covered many academic subjects. She also had to know the space shuttle inside and out. Ellen passed the training course. She became an astronaut in July 1991.

Ellen's first space shuttle mission was in April 1993. During the 9-day flight on the *Discovery*, Ellen worked to gather more information about the changes taking place in the ozone layer. This is the part of the atmosphere that protects the earth from the sun's harmful ultraviolet rays.

In November 1994, Ellen went on a second mission. It was a 10-day mission aboard the space shuttle *Atlantis*. Ellen used a remote robotic arm to retrieve a satellite that had been collecting information on the ozone layer. She did studies to learn more about the sun's energy cycle and how it affects the earth's climate.

Her third space shuttle flight began in May 1999. This was an historic trip. It was the first time the shuttle docked with the International Space Station. Ellen had to transfer two tons of supplies from the shuttle to the space station. In 2000, the first live crew was to live on the space station. They would need the supplies.

In April 2002, Ellen flew aboard the space shuttle *Atlantis* again. She stayed on the International Space Station for eleven days. She used the robotic arm to move crew members during three spacewalks.

When Ellen became an astronaut, she decided that she wanted to be a good role model for young people. She knew that being an astronaut put her in a position where students would listen to her. Ellen tries to show them that study and hard work will pay off.

Ellen spends a lot of time speaking at schools. She encourages young people, especially girls, to study math and science. She hopes that her success will show that anyone who works hard enough in school and on the job can succeed.

Ellen says, "I'm not trying to make every kid an astronaut. I want kids to think about a career and the preparation they'll need … I tell students that the opportunities I had were a result of having a good education. Education is what allows you to stand out."

Ellen Ochoa works hard. But she takes time to enjoy the beauty of life, too. Ellen took her flute along on the shuttle mission. Her music was surely a happy reminder of home.

Remembering the Facts

1. Why does Ellen credit her mother for her own success?

2. Why did Ellen turn down a scholarship to Stanford?

3. What musical instrument does Ellen play?

4. Why did Ellen get her pilot's license?

5. In what field does Ellen hold three patents?

6. What did Ellen study on the space shuttle?

7. Why is the ozone layer of the atmosphere important?

8. What is the message Ellen Ochoa brings when she speaks to students?

Understanding the Story

9. Ellen Ochoa's mother took college courses over a period of 20 years while she raised her family. Finally, she earned her college degree. Why do you think she was such a strong influence on Ellen?

10. Why do you think Ellen encourages girls to study math and science?

Getting the Main Idea

Why is Ellen Ochoa a good role model for the youth of today?

Applying What You've Learned

Imagine that you are in space aboard the space shuttle. Write a paragraph about your day in space.

Jaime Escalente

Math Teacher

Jaime Escalente was born in 1930 in Bolivia. His parents were teachers in a small Indian village.

Jaime's family life was not happy. His father drank too much and beat his wife. When Escalente was nine years old, his mother left his father. She moved her five children to La Paz, Bolivia.

When Jaime was 14, his mother sent him to a private high school. In school, Jaime was known for his jokes. He was also a good fighter. He usually tried to get out of doing his homework. But he loved math and science.

Jaime finished high school. He decided to train to become a teacher. When Jaime was in his second year of college, a local high school physics teacher died. Jaime was asked to take his place. At the same time, he worked to complete his teaching degree.

In 1954, Jaime got a job teaching physics at his old high school. He also taught part-time at two other schools.

Jaime Escalente was a tough teacher. He assigned his students 50 to 100 problems a night. A student who broke the rules might get another 200 problems. He pushed all his students to their limit. His motto was, "What is mediocre (low quality) is useless."

Jaime soon became known as a great teacher. His students won many awards. But teachers in Bolivia were not well paid. Jaime had to work three or four jobs. He decided to move his family to Los Angeles.

Jaime was in for a shock. California would not accept his Bolivian teaching degree. To teach in the United States, he would have to repeat college. That meant four years of college and one year of graduate study before he could teach.

He began taking night courses at Pasadena City College. To support his family, he took a job washing floors in a restaurant. It was not long until he became its chief cook.

It was slow going to school only part time. Then Jaime won a scholarship. Now he could go to school full time. He got his American teaching degree at the age of 43.

Jaime Escalente started to teach math at Garfield High School. This school was in the barrio of East Los Angeles. The students came from poor families. The school was overrun with gangs. Graffiti covered the walls. Trash was all over the school grounds. Most of the students did not finish high school.

Jaime went to work! On Saturdays he came to school and cleaned up his room. He and some students painted. He put up posters of the L.A. Lakers.

He went to work on his students, too. He pushed them hard. He decided that the math book was far too easy. He asked the principal for new books. He was told there was no money. After he said he would quit, money was found.

Jaime looked past the background of his students. He saw many of them had a lot of ability. He began teaching harder math courses. Finally, he added a course in calculus.

The first year he taught calculus, only five students passed the course. Everyone else dropped out.

The story that made Jaime Escalente famous involved the Advanced Placement exam for calculus. The Advanced Placement exam is a national test given at the end of the school year. Students across the country who pass the test get college credit for the course. The test is hard. Very few students in the country pass. But the first year Jaime taught calculus, two of his five students passed.

That was good. But Jaime knew he could do better. He scouted the lower grades for good students. Each year his calculus courses were a little larger. More of his students passed the Advanced Placement exam in calculus.

In 1982, 18 Garfield High students took the AP Calculus exam. *All* of the students passed. This kind of success was unheard of.

But the test correctors thought they saw a problem. Twelve of the students had solved one of the problems in the same way. They accused the students of cheating on the exam. The scores were thrown out. Jaime and his principal complained. Some of the students' parents complained, too.

Finally, the testers agreed that the students could retake the test. So in August, all the students took the test again. But it had been months since the last test. Would they remember their calculus well enough to pass?

They did! Again all the students passed. All won college credit for calculus. They had not cheated. They had solved the problems in the same way because that was how they had been taught.

The story hit newspapers across the country. No one could believe that a school like Garfield could have so many students pass the AP test. Most schools only had a few pass each year. Yet Garfield, in the barrio of East Los Angeles, had 18.

The reason was Jaime Escalente. He believed in his students. He kindly yet firmly insisted that they do the tough work he assigned. Anyone who did not work hard could expect a call to their parents. They would also get extra work before school, after school, and on weekends.

Jaime's classroom became a model. Visiting teachers and principals came to study his teaching methods.

The story of Jaime Escalente's life was shown in the hit movie *Stand and Deliver.* He was played by Edward James Olmos. The movie made Jaime Escalente the most famous math teacher in America.

In 2001, Escalente returned to his native Bolivia. There he continued teaching part time at the local university.

Jaime Escalente's new students know what to expect. One thing is for sure: They will work hard, and they will succeed. And they will always remember his rule:

"Determination + Hard Work + Discipline = The Way to Success."

Remembering the Facts

1. What were Jaime's two favorite subjects in school?

2. Why did Jaime decide to move to the United States from Bolivia?

3. What did Jaime have to do before he could teach in the United States?

4. Name three problems Jaime faced when he started teaching at Garfield High.

5. What is the purpose of taking an AP test?

6. Why did the test correctors think Jaime Escalente's students had cheated on the AP test?

7. Name the movie that tells Jaime Escalente's life story.

8. What three things make up Jaime Escalente's winning formula for success?

Understanding the Story

9. Explain Escalente's rule: "Determination + Hard Work + Discipline = The Way to Success."

10. Explain Escalente's motto: "What is mediocre is useless."

Getting the Main Idea

Why do you think Jaime Escalente is a good role model for the youth of today?

Applying What You've Learned

Choose a job that interests you. Make a list of ways a person with that job would need to use math at work.

Edward James Olmos

Activist Actor

Edward James Olmos has been called the best Hispanic-American actor today. Olmos is proof that with hard work you can become whatever you want to be.

Edward was born in East Los Angeles in 1947. His father was an immigrant from Mexico. His mother was a Mexican American.

When Edward was eight, his parents divorced. The three Olmos children were raised by their mother in a small house in East Los Angeles.

Edward Olmos wanted to escape poverty. He knew he must stay out of street gangs. He knew he must stay off drugs. He decided his way out would be baseball. He worked hard to improve. Finally, he won the Golden State batting championship. The discipline he learned in baseball stayed with him the rest of his life.

At the age of 15, Edward lost interest in baseball. He decided he wanted to be a singer. He took singing lessons. He taught himself to play the piano. Then he started a band called Eddie James and the Pacific Ocean. Edward was the lead singer.

The band got a nightly job at a club on Sunset Strip. During the day, Edward went to East Los Angeles City College.

Edward feared public speaking. He hoped to improve, so he signed up for a drama class. He liked it so much, he decided to become an actor.

Success in acting did not come right away. He had to work as a furniture mover to support his wife and two sons. Soon he landed some small parts in TV shows and movies. Usually, he played the role of the "bad guy."

In 1988, Edward played the role that changed his life as an actor. It was a part in *Zoot Suit*, a musical drama. It was the story of a group of Mexican-American youths wrongly convicted of a murder in Los Angeles in 1942. Edward played the role of El Pachuco, the narrator and star of the play. He delivered a powerful performance.

Zoot Suit took Los Angeles by storm. Suddenly, the city became aware of its Mexican-American community. The play was supposed to run for ten days. It ended up running for a year and a half. Then it moved to Broadway. Edward was nominated for a Tony award for his performance. Later, he starred in the movie version of the play.

El Pachuco is a symbol of the proud Chicano spirit that arose in California in the 1940s. The part was important to Edward because he was playing the first true-to-life Hispanic character ever seen on the American stage.

The TV series *Miami Vice* made Edward famous. For his work on the show, Edward won an Emmy for best supporting actor in 1985. He won a Golden Globe award in 1986. He was one of the first Hispanic actors to have a leading role on a long-lasting (five years) TV show. Many critics felt that Edward was the most interesting character in the entire series.

One of Edward's favorite roles was that of Jaime Escalente in the movie *Stand and Deliver*. Escalente was a math teacher in a gang-filled high school in East Los Angeles. He inspired 18 of his students to take and pass the Advanced Placement test in calculus. Along the way, Escalente taught his students to have pride in themselves. He taught them they could succeed in life.

Stand and Deliver was an important movie to the Hispanic community. It gave a message of hope to those living in poverty. It showed that belief in oneself and hard work are what it takes to succeed. Edward said, "The film is really about the triumph of the human spirit. It's about something we've lost—the joy of learning."

To play the part of Escalente, Edward spent hundreds of hours watching Escalente teach. He gained 40 pounds. He learned Escalente's speech patterns and mannerisms. For his work, he was nominated for an Academy Award for best actor.

Edward James Olmos has been in more than 70 movies and television shows. In his acting, he tries to show Hispanics in a positive, realistic way. A few of his outstanding performances were:

- *The Ballad of Gregorio Cortez* (1982)

- *Stand and Deliver* (1988)

- *American Me* (1992)

- *Menendez: A Murder in Beverly Hills* (1994)

- *The Burning Season* (1994)

- *My Family* (1995)

- *In the Time of Butterflies* (2001)

- *Walkout* (2006)

- *Battlestar Gallactica* (2004–2006)

Edward is also known for his public service. He has helped make peace between warring gangs in Los Angeles. He has worked with children with disabilities, and has spoken out against drug abuse.

Edward speaks at prisons and detention centers. He speaks on Indian reservations and at hospitals. He speaks at high schools. And he is in great demand at teachers' meetings. On average, he gives 150 talks a year.

He tells students that it is possible to improve their lives. He points to himself as an example. "I come from a dysfunctional family. I'm a minority. I have no natural talent. But I did it. If I can do it, anybody can do it. I take away all the excuses."

Edward practices what he preaches. In April 1992, riots broke out in Los Angeles. White police officers had been videotaped beating a black man, Rodney King. But a jury declared them innocent of the charges.

Angry mobs rioted. There was destruction of property all over the city. Edward was one of the first to offer his help to Mayor Tom Bradley.

Edward seemed to be everywhere during the riots. He appeared on TV, asking for peace. He talked to those whose property was destroyed. Finally, he picked up a broom and began sweeping. Soon hundreds of people had joined him in the cleanup effort.

This is what Edward James Olmos is all about. He is a great actor who shows Hispanics in a positive light. He speaks out on issues of our day. And he has been committed to public service for many years.

Remembering the Facts

1. How did Edward James Olmos first hope to escape his early life of poverty?

2. Why did Edward sign up for a drama class in college?

3. What was *Zoot Suit* about?

4. What TV series made Edward famous?

5. For which movie did Edward receive an Academy Award nomination?

6. How does Edward prove to students that they can improve their lives?

7. How did Edward volunteer during the 1992 riots?

8. Edward is well-known for his public service work. Name two places he has spoken.

Understanding the Story

9. Edward is in demand as a speaker. He is often scheduled two years in advance. Why do you think he is in such demand?

10. How has Edward helped the Hispanic community?

Getting the Main Idea

Why do you think Edward James Olmos is a good role model for the youth of today?

Applying What You've Learned

Imagine that you are on the scene of the Los Angeles riots in 1992. You are asked to give a message on TV to calm the people. What would you say to help stop the riots?

Judy Baca

Artist

The Tujunga Wash is a flood control canal of the Los Angeles River. In 1976, the Army Corps of Engineers had an unusual request. They wanted Judy Baca, a Mexican-American artist, to paint a mural on the walls.

The result was one of the most amazing urban art projects in the United States. Judy called it the *Great Wall of Los Angeles*. It is the largest outdoor mural in the world!

Judith Francisca Baca was born in 1946 in Los Angeles. She lived with her grandmother, mother, and two aunts. The family spoke only Spanish.

Judy's mother worked in a tire factory, so Judy was raised mostly by her grandmother. Judy did not know her musician father.

School was hard for Judy. She spoke English poorly. So, the teacher let her paint while the other children did their work. This was when Judy's love of painting began.

Judy graduated from high school in 1964. The next year she married. In 1969, she graduated from California State University in Northridge. Her degree was in art.

Her marriage ended. Judy returned to teach at her old high school. But she did not keep that job very long.

In the early 1970s, many young people were protesting the war in Vietnam. They felt we should not be sending our soldiers to fight in a civil war so far away.

Judy joined the peace movement. She and other teachers took part in marches against the war. Finally, the principal fired all the teachers who took part in anti-war activities. Judy was one of them.

Judy had to look for another job. She found one with the City of Los Angeles Cultural Affairs Division.

In her new job, Judy taught art in the city parks. She spent a lot of time with teenagers. Tattoos and graffiti were their favorite art forms.

Judy started a club called *Las Vistas Nuevas.* The teenagers in the group came from four rival gangs.

Judy got the teenagers to paint a mural in Hollenbeck Park. They learned to get along. They gave up the gangs. It was the first of many murals Judy would do with groups of teenagers.

Judy wanted to learn more about mural painting. She went to Mexico to study with famous mural painters there.

Murals are an old Mexican art form. This "art for the people" or "public art" is not kept in museums. Instead, these large paintings are done on the walls of buildings, on bridges, or on other large surfaces.

Judy returned to Los Angeles. She began the Citywide Mural Project. She brought kids of all races together to work on the project. More than 250 murals came out of this effort.

The largest of these was the *Great Wall.* This mural is actually a half-mile long! The mural tells about the history of California. It shows the many contributions made by different ethnic minority groups.

If you walk along the mural, you will see many things. Prehistoric animals roam a California tar pit. Spanish explorer Juan Cabrillo arrives by ship. Mexicans and Yankees fight over gold. Chinese workers build the railroad. Migrant workers work in the fields. Hungry people line up for food during the Depression. Japanese Americans are imprisoned during World War II. The freedom riders work for civil rights. These and many more events are pictured in the *Great Wall.*

The finished *Great Wall* is an amazing sight. But just as amazing is how it was created. The painting took the span of five summers to finish. Hundreds of kids of all ages and races worked on it.

Judy raised the money to do the work. She outlined what she wanted done. She hired some workers. And she asked kids to join in the work.

In 1976, Judy started the Social and Public Art Resource Center (SPARC). This art center brought artists, community groups, and young people together. They work to do murals and preserve public art.

In 1987, Judy began another large project. It was called *World Wall: A Vision of the Future Without Fear.* This mural was to be done by artists from around the world.

The *World Wall* was made so it could be taken apart and moved. It was made in pieces, each 10-feet high and 30-feet long. Judy painted seven of these panels with the help of teenagers.

Artists from other countries painted another seven panels. Judy asked the artists to show their idea of "the future without fear." New panels were added by artists in each country it visited.

Judy hopes that the work will spread her ideas of a world of peace—a world in which the contributions of all races are valued.

In 2000, Judy did a mural in the Denver Airport. It is called *Our Land's Memory.* It shows immigrants walking from Mexico to the United States hoping for a better life.

In 2002, Judy returned to the *Great Wall of Los Angeles.* Twenty years of rain, smog, and sun had damaged it. Judy worked to raise $500,000 to repair the wall. She also planned to add 40 more years of history to the wall.

Today, Judy teaches art at UCLA (University of California, Los Angeles). She is vice chair of UCLA's Cesar Chavez Center. She remains active in Hispanic-American affairs. She is a well-known spokesperson for her community.

Remembering the Facts

1. What is the name of the largest outdoor mural in the United States?

2. What story is told on this mural?

3. Why did Judy Baca choose to paint murals?

4. Why did Judy lose her job teaching high school art?

5. Name three events pictured on the *Great Wall of Los Angeles.*

6. Describe how the *Great Wall of Los Angeles* was created.

7. How was *The World Wall* created?

8. What project did Judy undertake in 2002?

Understanding the Story

9. How was Judy's career in public art still a kind of teaching career?

10. Judy Baca once said, "As artists, we have the power of spreading ideas." What do you think she meant by this?

Getting the Main Idea

Why do you think Judy Baca is a good role model for young people of today?

Applying What You've Learned

Make your own mural. Divide a piece of paper into six boxes. In each draw a picture showing something important in your life.

Sandra Cisneros

Author

Sandra Cisneros is a Mexican-American writer. She writes stories about Hispanic-American women. Sandra hopes that her success will open the door for many other Hispanic writers.

Sandra was born in 1954 in Chicago, Illinois. Her father was Mexican. Her mother was Mexican American.

Sandra had six brothers. She says she felt like she grew up with seven fathers telling her what to do.

In her early years, Sandra and her family moved many times. When her father became homesick for Mexico, they would go back to Mexico City. They always returned to Chicago, but to a different street, a different apartment, and a different school.

But all the neighborhoods they tried had one thing in common: They were poor, with vacant lots and burned-out buildings.

All this moving was hard on Sandra. She became very shy. She had few friends.

Sandra spent a lot of time by herself. She developed a strong love of reading. Books became her escape. Later, Sandra said that her aloneness "was good for a would-be writer. It allowed ... time to think ... to imagine ... to read and prepare."

Sandra learned to hide within herself. She became an observer of other people. She watched and remembered how they looked, how they talked, and what they did. She took notes in a spiral notebook she carried with her all the time. Later, she used her observations in her poetry and short stories.

In high school, one of her teachers asked her to read some of her stories to the class. The students loved her stories. Sandra gained confidence in her ability. She became editor of the school's literary magazine. Her nickname was "the poet."

Sandra's parents had little education. But they stressed education to their children. Her father worked as a carpenter. But he wanted more for his children. He often told them to learn to use their heads, not their hands.

So when Sandra wanted to go to college, her father agreed. He thought that college would be a good place for her to find a husband. Sandra had other ideas. At Loyola University she earned her degree in English. She hoped to become a writer.

Her talent earned her a spot in the famous University of Iowa Writers' Workshop. Here she studied among writers from the best schools in the country. The workshop proved to be a turning point in her life as a writer.

She soon realized that she had little in common with the other students at the workshop. She felt out of place, almost foreign. Later she described herself as a "yellow weed among the city's cracks." Her classmates had been bred as "hothouse flowers."

One day in class, students were telling about the houses where they had grown up. As she listened, Sandra realized she had no such house in her memories. As they talked, Sandra suddenly knew why she felt different from the other students. She *was* different in her race and culture. She was a Mexican-American woman.

At that moment, she accepted herself for who she was. She realized her voice was one of a kind. She had found herself. She would write about things her classmates could never write about.

From this awakening, her first book was born. *The House on Mango Street* is the story of Esperanza, a young girl growing up in a poor Hispanic neighborhood in Chicago. Through her eyes, the reader sees the lives of the people living there. In the course of the book, Esperanza learns to understand both herself and her culture.

But Esperanza wants a better life for herself. By the end of the book, she decides how she will escape her poverty: through her writing. But at the close of the book, she is reminded that leaving Mango Street does not mean leaving who she is. In fact, the story of Esperanza is the story of Sandra Cisneros herself.

This book got great reviews. Yet Sandra was unable to make a living from her writing. She worked at odd jobs, trying to scrape out a living. This was the low point of her life.

Sandra went back to earn her master's degree. She taught for three years in a high school in Chicago. She earned a variety of fellowships. During this time, she wrote a collection of poetry called *My Wicked, Wicked Ways.*

Meanwhile, in New York City, a literary agent had read *The House on Mango Street.* She was so moved by the book that she tried to track down Sandra. She wanted to help her publish more books.

It took nearly four years for the two women to get together. But finally it worked out. This led to the publication, in 1991, of Sandra's third book, *Women Hollering Creek and Other Stories.* The title story has been called one of the great short stories in American literature. The book was selected as a *New York Times* noteworthy book of the year.

In this book, Sandra talks about the lives of Hispanic women. All of her characters are strong women. They are women of different ages, races, and situations telling their stories. Her fourth book, *Loose Woman*, was published in 1994.

In 2002, Sandra published *Caramelo.* It was selected as a notable book of the year by several major newspapers.

Sandra Cisneros is now recognized as a major talent. *The House on Mango Street* is being read in schools and colleges across the country. Over three million copies are in print.

Today, Sandra lives in San Antonio, Texas. Her hobby is collecting vintage clothing. She says that she lives "in a violet house filled with many creatures, great and small."

Sandra hopes to give something back to the Hispanic community. While she has left her childhood of poverty behind, it is still a part of her. As one of her characters in *The House on Mango Street* tells Esperanza:

"You will always be Esperanza. You will always be Mango Street. You can't erase what you know. You can't forget who you are. You must remember to come back. For the ones who cannot leave as easily as you."

Sandra Cisneros will never leave the Hispanic community. She is herself a symbol of the Mexican-American woman. Through her writing, her story is being heard at last.

Remembering the Facts

1. Why did the Cisneros family move so often?

2. Why did Sandra Cisneros develop a love for reading?

3. Why did Sandra's shyness help her as a writer?

4. How did Sandra come to realize that she had a unique voice as a writer?

5. What was the name of Sandra's first book?

6. What does Sandra talk about in this book?

7. Why does Sandra say that her childhood of poverty will always be a part of her?

Understanding the Story

8. Why do you think it would be important for anyone who wants to become a writer to read a lot?

9.   Why do you think *The House on Mango Street* is required reading in many schools?

10.   What do you think is meant by these lines from *The House on Mango Street?*

      "You will always be Esperanza. You will always be Mango Street. You can't erase what you know. You can't forget who you are."

Getting the Main Idea

Why do you think Sandra Cisneros is a good role model for the youth of today?

Applying What You've Learned

Make a list of events, places, and people who were important in your early life—things that make you different from everyone else.

Roberto Clemente

Baseball Player

Roberto Clemente was born in 1934 in a small town near San Juan, Puerto Rico. He was the youngest of seven children. His father was the foreman of a sugar plantation.

Even before he started school, Roberto loved to play baseball. He started with softball. Later, he played in a city league. He played so much baseball he sometimes forgot to eat.

When he wasn't playing baseball, he was listening to games on the radio. Hour after hour, he squeezed a hard rubber ball. He hoped to make his arm stronger. It must have worked. Roberto had one of the best arms in baseball.

In high school, Roberto played baseball. He was also on the school track team. He was thought to be a sure bet for the 1952 Olympic track team. But baseball got in the way.

One day Roberto was playing ball at the park. He was using an old, torn fielder's mitt. The owner of the Santurce Crabbers (a winter league team) saw him. He was amazed at the boy's skills. On the spot, he offered Roberto a job. He signed a contract for $500—and a new glove.

A year later, in 1953, a scout for the Brooklyn Dodgers spotted Roberto. The scout wanted to sign Roberto that day. But his father said no. His son must finish high school first. He wanted his son to become an engineer. That was looking less likely all the time.

When Roberto finished high school, nine teams wanted him. The Dodgers offered him $10,000 to sign with them. That was the largest amount ever offered a Hispanic player.

Roberto accepted the offer. Hours later, the Milwaukee Braves offered him $30,000.

Roberto didn't know what to do. He had not signed any papers with the Dodgers. But he had agreed to the first offer. He asked his parents for advice. His mother said, "If you gave the word, you keep the word." To the Clementes, honor was more important than money. So Roberto signed with the Dodgers.

Roberto began his career in the minor leagues. His first year, he played for the Dodgers' farm team in Montreal, Canada.

His first year was not happy. He did not speak much English. Customs and food in Canada were strange to him. And he was a black Hispanic in a mostly white country. He felt like an outsider.

Roberto soon had a health problem, too. Baseball bats in the 1950s were thick and heavy. But a new lighter bat had come out. Players could hit farther with the new bat. Roberto decided to try one out. He picked up a light bat and swung hard. That was a big mistake. He hurt his back.

Then in 1954, a drunk driver hit Roberto's car. Again, his back was hurt. Many times after that he had to sit out from games. When he did play, he was often in pain.

In 1954, Roberto was drafted by the Pittsburgh Pirates. He was the number one draft choice in the country. His first year with the Pirates, the team finished last. But Roberto played well, batting .360.

After games, Roberto had no place to go. So he went down and talked to the fans before they left the stadium. It was the start of a long-lasting friendship with the Pirates fans.

With Roberto's help, the Pirates improved. He was rewarded with a big increase in pay. He used much of it to buy a new home for his parents.

During the winter of 1957, Roberto was in the United States Marines. For six months, he worked long hours. The work helped his weak back. When he went back to the Pirates for the 1958 season, his back was strong again.

The 1960 season was one of Roberto's best. That year the Pirates won the National League championship. It was the first time they had won in 33 years. The team went on to win the World Series against the New York Yankees.

With all his fame, Roberto Clemente never forgot his roots in Puerto Rico. Every year after baseball season ended, he returned home. He spent the winter working with kids who wanted to play baseball.

In 1963, Roberto married Vera Zabala. They built a new home near Roberto's parents in Puerto Rico. Over the years they had three sons.

Roberto's career was booming. In 1966, he won the Most Valuable Player award for the National League. He had become the star of the Pirates.

In 1970, the Pirates honored Roberto by holding Roberto Clemente Night. Thousands of people came to cheer for him. He was given a gift of $6,000. Few people ever knew that Roberto gave the check to the Children's Hospital in Pittsburgh that very night. In fact, he often gave large amounts of money to charity. But he always kept it a secret.

Again in 1971, the Pirates, led by Roberto Clemente, won the World Series. Roberto was named the outstanding player of the series.

In the spring of 1972, Roberto made his 3,000th hit. Only ten other players in the history of baseball had equaled that feat. It would be Roberto's last regular season hit of his life.

On December 22, 1972, an earthquake hit Nicaragua. Thousands were killed. The capital city of Managua was nearly destroyed.

Roberto Clemente began setting up a Puerto Rican relief effort. He began collecting food, clothes, and medical supplies.

There were rumors that planeloads of supplies were being stolen when they arrived in Nicaragua. Roberto decided to fly on the supply plane to make sure those who needed help got it.

It was New Year's Eve. Roberto canceled his party plans. He boarded the plane for Nicaragua. Shortly after takeoff, the plane exploded. It plunged into the ocean. There were no survivors. Roberto Clemente's body has never been found.

Puerto Rico had lost its greatest hero. Baseball had lost one of its top stars. Here are some of Roberto Clemente's achievements:

- 4 National League batting championships

- 3,000 hits in the major leagues

- Lifetime batting average of .317

- National League's Most Valuable Player, 1966 and 1971

- 12 Golden Glove awards for fielding excellence

- 1st Hispanic American to enter the Baseball Hall of Fame

Roberto Clemente was a great ballplayer. But he did all he could for those in need as well. He once said, "Any time you have the chance to do something for someone else and you don't do it, you are wasting your time on this earth." That was how Roberto lived his life. And that is why he was much more than a great ballplayer. He is remembered by many as a hero.

Remembering the Facts

1. With what team did Roberto sign his first contract (for $500)?

2. Why did Roberto sign a contract with the Dodgers when the Braves offered him more money?

3. Why was Roberto unhappy in his first years of professional baseball?

4. What two events caused Roberto's years of back pain?

5. What team drafted Roberto in 1954 as its number one draft choice?

6. What did Roberto do in the winter when baseball was over?

7. Why did Roberto go on the plane with the medical supplies for Nicaragua?

8. Name three awards won by Roberto during his career.

Understanding the Story

9. Why do you think Roberto Clemente is a hero to many Puerto Ricans?

10. When Roberto gave gifts to charity, he always kept it a secret. What do you think that tells about the kind of man he was?

Getting the Main Idea

Why do you think Roberto Clemente is a good role model for the young people of today?

Applying What You've Learned

Imagine that you are in charge of organizing relief efforts for victims of an earthquake. Make a list of things the victims would need most.

Henry B. Gonzalez

U.S. Congressman

Henry B. Gonzalez was the first Mexican American to be elected to Congress. He was a U.S. Representative from Texas for 38 years.

In 1953, Henry decided to run for the city council of San Antonio. He went to the city leaders and asked for their help. Every one of them advised him not to run. "A Mexican cannot win," they told him. But Henry did run. And he was elected to the city council.

Later, he decided to run for the Texas State Senate. Again, he was told that a Mexican could not win state office. But in 1956, he won that race, too. That made him the first Mexican American in 110 years to be elected to the Texas State Senate.

Henry did not stop there. In 1961, he ran for the United States Congress. He won 55% of the vote. In those days, the voting rights of African Americans and Hispanics were restricted. So, it was clear that many white Texans had voted for him. It was an amazing victory!

Henry Barbosa Gonzalez was born in 1916 in San Antonio, Texas. He was one of six children.

Henry's father had been the mayor of Mapimi, a village in northern Mexico. During the 1910 Revolution he was forced to flee his home. He went to San Antonio. He became the editor of *La Prensa*. This was the only newspaper written in Spanish in the United States.

Henry grew up in a home that was full of talk of politics and ideas. His parents stressed the importance of a good education. From an early age, Henry loved to read. The public library was his second home.

But Henry had problems in school. To begin with, his family spoke only Spanish in their home. He reached school age without knowing a word of English.

When it was time for him to start school, his father had to drag him out of the house. In class he was one of a handful of Mexican-American children. He was so frightened he didn't speak a word for months. But by the end of the year he had learned to speak English.

Henry graduated from Thomas Jefferson High School. He went on to college. He earned a law degree from St. Mary's University School of Law in 1943.

But Henry never practiced law. He worked for a Spanish-English translation service for a few years. He worked on housing programs in San Antonio. During World War II, he worked for army intelligence.

When he was elected to the state senate, Henry fought for minority rights. He worked for programs to replace slums with better housing. He was against a sales tax that would have hurt the poor.

Henry set a state record for the longest filibuster. (A filibuster is a long speech used to delay a bill coming up for a vote.) Once, the Texas State Senate was trying to pass ten racial segregation bills. Henry and another senator filibustered for 36 hours.

After he had spoken for 22 hours, Henry said, "I have seen the effects of segregation firsthand for many years. If we fear long enough, we hate. And if we hate long enough, we fight. If a bill violates the rights of even one person, then it has to be struck down." Only one of the ten bills was passed.

Henry Gonzalez was a close friend of President John F. Kennedy. On November 22, 1963, Henry was with Kennedy on a trip to Dallas. Just before they got off the plane, Henry joked, "I'm taking my risks. I haven't got my steel vest on." Just minutes later, while riding into Dallas, President Kennedy was shot and killed.

Henry suspected that Kennedy's assassin had not acted alone. He asked Congress to look into the case. He also wanted the assassination of Dr. Martin Luther King Jr. investigated.

In 1981, Henry became chairman of the House Banking Subcommittee on Housing. He pushed hard for more low-income housing. He finally got the Affordable Housing Act passed in 1990. This act helps low-income families to buy homes.

In 1988, Henry became chairman of the House Banking, Finance, and Urban Affairs Committee. His first task was to handle the savings and loan crisis. A savings and loan is a type of bank that lends money for home buying.

The head of one savings and loan had tried to bribe several U.S. senators. Some savings and loans were guilty of fraud. Others were not managing their money the right way.

Henry got a bill passed to bail out some failing savings and loans. Then he set up tighter rules for how they could do business. Stricter laws for regular banks were set up, too.

In 1999, Henry retired from Congress. His son, Charlie Gonzales, succeeded him. Henry Gonzales died on November 28, 2000 in San Antonio.

In all the years he was in Congress, Henry was known for his honesty and independence. He once said, "I walked through the mud of San Antonio politics. I walked through the mud of state politics in Texas. And for 30 years, I've walked through the mud in Washington, DC, and I still haven't gotten the tips of my shoes dirty." Henry B. Gonzalez was an honest man.

In Texas, Henry B. (as he is known) is a hero. He was so popular that he was reelected to Congress 19 times.

Remembering the Facts

1. What job did Henry B. Gonzalez hold from 1961 to 1999?

2. Why did Henry have trouble when he started school?

3. Name two things Henry B. Gonzalez worked for while in the Texas State Senate.

4. How did Henry bring nine out of ten segregationist bills to defeat?

5. With which U.S. president was Henry close friends?

6. What law did Henry get passed when he was chairman of the House Banking Subcommittee on Housing?

7. What was the first crisis Henry had to handle as chairman of the House Banking, Finance, and Urban Affairs Committee?

8. What kind of reputation does Henry B. Gonzalez have in Washington, DC?

Understanding the Story

9. Why do you think Henry B. Gonzalez was so popular in his home state of Texas?

10. Explain Gonzalez's statement "For 30 years, I've walked through the mud in Washington, DC, and I still haven't gotten the tips of my shoes dirty."

Getting the Main Idea

Why do you think Henry B. Gonzalez is a good role model for the youth of today?

Applying What You've Learned

Write a paragraph about a political issue of today that you think Henry would be involved with if he were alive.

Roberto Goizueta

Chairman of the Coca-Cola Company

There are few Cuban Americans in the top ranks of business. One of them was Roberto Goizueta. He was chairman and chief executive of the Coca-Cola Company for 16 years.

Roberto led the company to new highs in sales. Coca-Cola is now America's sixth most valuable public company. Today it has 372 drink products it sells around the world. Of these, the most popular is still Coca-Cola.

Roberto Goizueta was born in Havana, Cuba, in 1931. His father was a businessman in the sugar industry. Roberto grew up in a wealthy home.

At the age of 18, Roberto came to the United States. He went to a private high school in Connecticut.

Roberto didn't know a word of English. A year later he spoke English well. He learned "after many sleepless nights studying the dictionary."

Because he was rich, his classmates thought he would be spoiled. They were wrong. Roberto was a hard worker. He had good values. He finished high school first in his class.

Roberto went on to Yale. He earned a degree in chemical engineering in 1954. Then he returned to Cuba. His father wanted him to work in the sugar business with him. But Roberto wanted a different job. He answered a newspaper ad. The ad read, "American company seeks a bilingual chemical engineer." Roberto was hired as a chemist at the Coca-Cola plant in Havana, Cuba.

When Fidel Castro came to power in Cuba, the country became communist. By 1960, Castro was taking over businesses and property. Many people were thrown in jail for little or no reason.

Roberto, his wife, and three children fled Cuba in 1961. They left everything behind. When they arrived in the United States, they had $40 and 100 shares of Coca-Cola stock. At first, they all lived in a motel room. A curtain divided the parents' and childrens' beds.

Roberto later said, "You cannot explain that experience to any person. All of a sudden you don't own anything. It builds a feeling of not much regard for material things."

Shortly after the Goizuetas came to the United States, the government of Cuba took over the Coke plant there. Roberto Goizueta kept working for Coca-Cola. The company gave him an office in an airport hotel in Miami.

In 1961, the company moved him to the Bahamas. He worked on the island of Nassau. He was the area chemist for Coke in the Caribbean.

In 1964, he was moved to company headquarters in Atlanta, Georgia. He became vice president for research and development. At age 35, he was Coca-Cola's youngest vice president ever. Roberto and his wife became U.S. citizens in 1969.

In the 1970s, Robert Woodruff noticed the work that Roberto was doing. Woodruff had been chairman of Coke for many years. Woodruff became a mentor to Roberto. Roberto began to advance rapidly up the ladder. In 1980, he was named president of the company.

Some people were not happy when Roberto was put in charge. He was only 48. There were older and more experienced people in line for the job. Other people did not like the fact that Roberto had come from Cuba. He spoke English well, but he spoke it with a heavy accent. How could such a man lead the all-American company Coca-Cola?

Roberto Goizueta soon proved himself. When he took office, Pepsi was selling better than Coke in grocery stores. He needed to boost

Coke's sales. The company chose a new slogan: "Coke Is It!" A new product came out in 1982: Diet Coke®. This quickly became the country's best-selling diet soft drink. Coke moved ahead of Pepsi in sales.

Roberto's least successful idea was the introduction of "New Coke." The original Coca-Cola had been developed by John Pemberton (an Atlanta pharmacist) in 1886. But in 1984, researchers at Coke thought they had come up with a drink that tasted better. The new Coke was sweeter and smoother. Coke started selling the new drink. They said they would lock the old recipe up in a bank vault and never use it again.

People all across the country were upset. The Coca-Cola company received thousands of calls a day. No one could believe that Coke had been changed. Coke was an American tradition. One man said that changing Coke was like making grass purple!

It took just a month for Roberto Goizueta to get the message from the American people. "We want our Coke back!" So, he said that from then on there would be two Cokes: new Coke and old Coke. The old Coke was called Coca-Cola Classic.

New Coke had been a big mistake. But it turned out all right in the end. There were two Cokes. And Coca-Cola was selling more soft drinks than ever. (New Coke is no longer sold.)

By the 1990s, Coke was far outselling Pepsi in the United States. Worldwide it was outselling its rivals four to one. Most of the credit for this went to Roberto.

Company employees liked Roberto's leadership style. One said, "He has this way of improving your performance without your knowing it. When you see him so active and so interested in everything, you have no choice but to be the same."

Roberto worked to increase cultural diversity in Coca-Cola's leadership. He did this very well. Later he said, "We view ourselves as an international company that just happens to be based in Atlanta. We have as many accents here as in the United Nations."

Coca-Cola was a major sponsor of the 1996 Olympic Games in Atlanta. Coke had been involved in every Olympics since 1928. "I'd like to buy the world a Coke" became a theme song. It was a fitting theme for a drink loved around the world.

Today, Coke is sold in nearly every country. (Cuba is not one of them.) A recent survey found that Coca-Cola was the best-known trademark in the world. In 2003, a new slogan was introduced: "Coca-Cola…Real."

On October 18, 1997, Roberto Goizueta died in Atlanta at the age of 65. The Cuban immigrant had led one of the world's best known companies to even greater success.

Remembering the Facts

1. Why did the Goizueta family leave Cuba in 1961?

2. How did Robert Woodruff help Roberto Goizueta?

3. What job did Roberto get in 1980?

4. Why were some people unhappy when Roberto took over the company?

5. What was the biggest marketing mistake made by Roberto?

6. How was this marketing mistake corrected?

7. What major event did Coca-Cola sponsor in 1996?

8. Where is the Coca-Cola company located?

Understanding the Story

9.   How do you think Roberto "led by example"?

10.   Why do you think people were so upset when Coca-Cola changed its formula in 1984?

Getting the Main Idea

Why do you think Roberto Goizueta is a good role model for the youth of today?

Applying What You've Learned

Think of a new slogan for Coca-Cola. Design a poster featuring the new slogan.

Antonia Novello

Surgeon General

Antonia Novello was the 14th Surgeon General of the United States. She was the first woman to hold that job. She was the first Hispanic (and the first Puerto Rican) to be the nation's "first doctor."

Antonia Novello was born in on August 23, 1944 in Fajardo, Puerto Rico. Her parents divorced when she was young. Antonia was raised by her mother.

Antonia was born with an abnormally large intestine. She was often ill. Every year she spent at least two weeks in the hospital. Surgery could have fixed the problem, but she was not able to have the operation until she was 18.

Antonia's doctors were her heroes as a child. She knew from an early age that she wanted to become a pediatrician (a doctor for children). She never told anyone her dream. She was afraid it would sound "too good of a notion."

With her mother's support, Antonia made her dream come true. She went to the University of Puerto Rico to study medicine. In 1970, she became a medical doctor.

The same year, she married Dr. Joe Novello. He was a flight surgeon in the United States Navy. The couple moved to Ann Arbor, Michigan.

Antonia Novello was an intern and resident at University of Michigan Medical Center. There were very few women doctors in the 1970s. Most people thought she was a nurse! But Antonia's skill soon won them over. She was named "Intern of the Year" in 1971. She was the first woman to get this honor.

Antonia's favorite aunt died of kidney failure at age 32. So Antonia decided to specialize in childhood kidney disorders. She studied at Georgetown University in Washington, DC.

In 1976, Antonia opened an office. She began work as a pediatrician. A few years later, she decided the work did not suit her. She said, "When the pediatrician cries as much as the parents of the patients do, then you know it's time to get out." She was upset that so many patients did not get the help they needed because of hospital and government rules. She decided she could make more of a contribution working for the government.

Antonia earned a master's degree in public health from Johns Hopkins University. She went to work for the public health service. She rose quickly through the ranks. She worked with the United States Congress on health-related issues.

She worked on the National Organ Procurement and Transplantation Act of 1984. In 1986, she became deputy director of the National Institute of Child Health and Human Development. She worked to fight childhood AIDS.

In 1989, President George H.W. Bush nominated Antonia to be the surgeon general. She was confirmed by the Senate. On March 9, 1990, she became the nation's 14th Surgeon General. Her oath of office was given by another "first," Justice Sandra Day O'Connor, the first woman on the U.S. Supreme Court.

As surgeon general, Antonia's job was to protect the health of the American people. She chose four areas she would emphasize during her term of office. These were teenage drinking, teen smoking, AIDS, and childhood vaccinations.

Antonia said alcohol is a big problem for America's youth. At least eight million underage students drink alcohol. At least half a million are alcoholics.

Antonia said alcohol ads send kids a false message. They make drinking look like the "key to fun and a wonderful and carefree lifestyle." Antonia worked for a ban on alcohol ads targeting young people. She asked for more alcohol education in schools.

Another of Antonia's targets was tobacco companies. She said tobacco ads are aimed at the young. In 1992, she singled out the cartoon character Joe Camel. One study showed that 91% of six-year-olds knew that Joe Camel sells cigarettes. The Marlboro Man ads show smokers as strong and independent. Antonia asked tobacco companies to stop ads that appeal to those under 18.

Antonia also stressed AIDS education. She tried to spread the message of how to protect oneself from AIDS.

During her term as surgeon general, Antonia Novello made no secret of her special concern for America's children. She decorated her office with Cabbage Patch dolls. She had children's artwork on the walls. She made time to visit children in hospitals.

In 1993, Antonia stepped down from her position as surgeon general. She served as the United Nations Children's Fund (UNICEF) Special Representative for Health and Nutrition from 1993 to 1996.

In 1996, she became Visiting Professor of Health Policy and Nutrition at Johns Hopkins. In 1999, she became Commissioner of Health of the state of New York.

In 2006, she was asked to run for the United States Senate from the state of New York. She decided not to run. That same year she was a finalist for *Hispanic Business* magazine's Woman of the Year award.

Antonia Novello's motto is "Good science, good sense." She tried to make good sense in her public health campaigns. She hoped people would listen and make changes for a healthier life. She has made important contributions to the health of children and women. And she is an excellent role model.

Remembering the Facts

1. What "firsts" did Antonia Novello make when she became surgeon general?

2. Why did Antonia decide to become a doctor?

3. Why did she decide to work for the public health service?

4. What is the job of the surgeon general?

5. Name four issues Antonia was concerned about as surgeon general.

6. Why did Antonia fight against alcohol and tobacco ads that targeted the young?

7. How did working for UNICEF fit her interests?

Understanding the Story

8. Why do you think Antonia Novello focused so much of her work as surgeon general on the problems of young people?

9. Why do you think Antonia kept her dream of being a doctor a secret when she was growing up?

10. Why do you think Antonia decided to fight the tobacco industry?

Getting the Main Idea

Why do you think Antonia Novello is a good role model for young people of today?

Applying What You've Learned

Find an ad for an alcohol or tobacco product. Write a paragraph explaining how the ad tries to make drinking or smoking appealing.

José Feliciano

Singer

José Feliciano was born in Lares, Puerto Rico in 1945. He was the second of eleven boys born to a poor farmer.

José's father did not succeed as a farmer. So the family moved to New York City when José was five years old. They lived in a ghetto called Spanish Harlem.

The family was poor. But José had a bigger problem. He had been born blind.

José was not allowed to join the street games played by other children. He spent much time at home by himself. He filled his time listening to the radio. Singers became his childhood heroes.

José remembers using a tin cracker can as a drum at the age of three. By six, he had taught himself to play the accordion. He played the same record over and over. Then he figured out how to make the same sounds on his instrument.

By the age of eight, José had taught himself to play the guitar. Again, he used a handful of records as his guide. He practiced 14 hours a day.

When he was nine, he began performing in public. His first job was at a theater in Spanish Harlem. José was very small. His father had to pick him up so the crowd could see him.

Times were hard for the Feliciano family. When José was 17, his father lost his job. José quit school to help earn money. He played wherever he could. Afterwards, he would pass around a hat.

It was not easy for him to get jobs at first. So, he thought of a trick. He would ask coffeehouse managers if they would listen to him sing. Most of them said "no." (They knew nothing about him.)

Then José would ask if he could tune his guitar before he left. The managers could not turn down that request. Of course, the guitar would already be in tune. José would pull it out and play beautifully. Often, he would be hired.

José began to gain a following among folk music lovers in New York City. Soon he was playing at some of the better known clubs.

José was only 17 when he got his big break. He was playing in a club in Greenwich Village. An executive from RCA Records was visiting the club to hear another act. He heard José instead. He wasted no time in signing the young man.

During the next five years, José made records in Spanish. These were for the Latin American market. He toured Europe, Central America, and South America. He became very popular among Spanish-speaking people. He even had his own Spanish language TV show. This show was shown all over Latin America.

José was a major recording artist in Latin America before he hit the U.S. charts. His hit album *Feliciano!* zoomed to the top of the charts in 1968. The single "Light My Fire" was the number one single in 1968. Both earned a gold record that year.

By the end of 1968, José was a star in the United States as well. He appeared on almost every major TV show. And he starred in several of his own TV specials.

In 1968, José became the first person to put his own spin on the national anthem during a sports event. He had been asked to sing "The Star-Spangled Banner" to open the fifth game of the 1968 World Series. He chose to do it in a Spanish soul style.

Many people were upset. They couldn't believe that he dared to sing the national anthem in such a way. In fact, many radio stations stopped playing his records in protest. Other people loved it. But for the first time, the national anthem (Feliciano style) was a Top 40 hit.

In 1971, José married. He and his wife Susan have three children.

José Feliciano is a rare artist. Besides the guitar, he plays the bass, banjo, and keyboard. He plays the harmonica, the mandolin, and the timbales. He also plays the piano, the organ, and the bongos.

He sings rock 'n roll and blues. He sings folk and Latin-American music. And he sings in seven different languages.

José Feliciano is always in demand. He has played for top symphony orchestras around the world. He has appeared on major TV shows and has done a number of his own specials. The three songs for which he is best known are "Light My Fire," "*Che Sera*," and "*Feliz Navidad*."

Critics worldwide have called José the "greatest living guitarist." He's been awarded over 45 gold and platinum records. He has won six Grammy awards. New York City renamed Public School 155 in East Harlem the "José Feliciano Performing Arts School."

José Feliciano is known as an Ambassador of Good Will around the world. He says, "I'll never forget where I came from or the people who helped my family or me along the way." He is quick to help causes he believes are important. He does 20 to 30 benefit concerts a year for organizations that serve the blind.

José has been loved by his fans around the world for 40 years. But he feels as if his career is just beginning. After all, he has a whole new generation of listeners. He feels that he is just beginning to share his music with the world.

José says that hard work is the "magic" ingredient toward success in any field. He says, "You can make it in music if you give it everything you've got and make sure it's the only thing on your mind." If you listen to his music, you will know he gives it all he's got. José says that music still gives him the same happiness it did when he was a child.

The name *Feliciano* means "the happy one" in Spanish. He has lived his life with a positive attitude, in spite of his handicap. Through his music, he has also given happiness to millions around the world.

Remembering the Facts

1. What two handicaps did José Feliciano have to overcome?

2. How did José get jobs at coffeehouses at first?

3. How did José get his big break?

4. Where did José gain fame before he became known in the United States?

5. Name the hit single that sent José to the top of the record charts in the United States.

6. José Feliciano plays many instruments. But he is best known for his skill on which instrument?

7. What does José say is the way to success in any field?

8. What does the name *Feliciano* mean in Spanish?

Understanding the Story

9. In 1968, José was the first person to sing the national anthem in a nontraditional way. Why do you think so many people were upset?

10. What effect do you think his blindness had on José's development of his talent?

Getting the Main Idea

Why do you think José Feliciano is a good role model for the youth of today?

Applying What You've Learned

Design a poster to advertise an upcoming José Feliciano concert in your area. Use facts from the story on your poster.

Ileana Ros-Lehtinen

U.S. Representative

In 1982, Ileana Ros-Lehtinen was the first Cuban-American woman to win election to the Florida state legislature. In 1989, she was the first Cuban-American woman to be elected to the United States Congress. She was also the first Hispanic-American to hold this office.

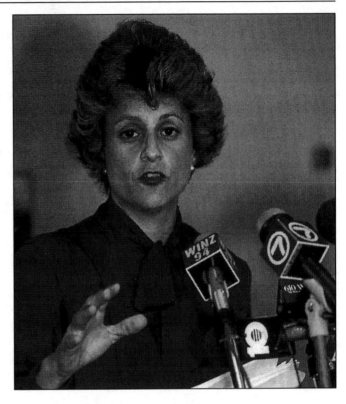

As a U.S. Representative, Ileana works for all Hispanic Americans. But she wants to represent all the people of her district.

Ileana Ros-Lehtinen was born in 1952 in Havana, Cuba. Her father was an accountant.

The Ros family lived a pleasant life. Then Fidel Castro came to power. Like many other Cubans, the Ros family fled to Miami in 1960. They left behind their home and all they owned.

There were many Cuban exiles in Miami. They all hoped that Castro would not stay in power long. Groups of exiles gathered at the Ros home nightly. They plotted ways to overthrow Castro. Then they would be able to go back to Cuba. Ileana remembers her home being "like a camp, full of people all day."

But it soon became clear that things in Cuba were not going to get better anytime soon. Ileana's parents decided that they would raise their children as Americans. They thought it wasn't fair to raise them without knowing which country they belonged to. Mr. Ros said, "This is going to be their country, and they should love it!"

It was no surprise that Ileana developed a strong desire to serve her country. She had lost her native land to communism. So she takes democracy very seriously.

Ileana graduated from Miami-Dade County Community College in 1972. She earned a degree in English from Florida International University in 1975. She also earned a master's degree in educational leadership. In 2004, she earned a doctorate in higher education from the University of Miami.

Ileana became a teacher. She founded her own private school, Eastern Academy. She was the principal of the school for ten years.

Ileana has always loved politics. So it was natural for her to run for the Florida state legislature. She ran and won. From 1982 to 1986, she was a state representative. Then she was a state senator until 1989.

While in the legislature, she met her future husband, Dexter Lehtinen. He was also a state senator. The couple later had two children. They also raised his two children from a previous marriage.

In 1989, the popular longtime U.S. Congressman Claude Pepper died. A special election was held to fill his seat. Ileana, a Republican, ran against Democrat Gerald Richman. It ended up being a bitter race.

The problems began when the Republican national chairman said that since the district was 50 percent Cuban, it was important to elect a Cuban American to the job. To this, Richman reportedly answered, "This is an American seat." Many Cuban Americans in Miami were upset by this remark. It sounded to them as if Richman was saying that they were not real Americans.

Ileana received 90 percent of the Hispanic-American vote. Most of the whites and African Americans voted for Richman. But in the end, Ileana was the new congresswoman from Florida's 18th District. Her election showed how powerful the Cuban-American vote had become in Florida.

In her victory speech, Ileana said she would start working to heal the wounds caused by the campaign. During her speech, she suddenly switched from English to Spanish. She did this to show those listening to her in Cuba what a democracy was all about.

She is well liked in her district because she spends most of her time helping local voters. Her office helps people with such things as getting food stamps or immigration papers.

Ileana feels that service to the people of her district is the most important part of her job in Congress. She sees herself as a middle person between the voter and the government. This approach has brought her a loyal following in her district.

Congresswoman Ros-Lehtinen serves on the Committee on International Relations. Currently she is the Chair of the Middle East and Central Asia subcommittee. She also serves on the Committee for Government Reform. She works on the subcommittee for National Security, Emerging Threats, and International Relations.

She supports bilingual education. She is for a seven-day waiting period to buy a handgun. She also favors tough sentences for drug dealers.

Like most Cuban Americans, Ileana is a strong opponent of Fidel Castro. She hopes that one day Cuba will again be a democracy.

Ileana Ros-Lehtinen has worked hard to help her district of South Florida. She has worked to bring $25 million in federal money to clean and dredge the Miami River. She has gotten $40 million to dredge the Port of Miami. (This was so it could serve big ships.) She has also helped expand the Miami International Airport.

Ileana has worked to protect the Florida Keys. She has secured $35 million in federal funds to make sure the waters of the Keys are clean and healthy. She is also a supporter of the Everglades cleanup project. This is one of the largest environmental projects ever undertaken in our country.

Ileana Ros-Lehtinen has been influential in foreign policy. She is especially interested in Latin American and Cuban issues. She supported the 1992 Cuban Democracy Act. The act speaks out against human rights violations in Cuba. It prohibits U.S. companies from trading with Cuba. A 1996 act charged penalties against companies that traded with Cuba. A 2000 act allowed the sale of medicine and food to Cuba. It also tightened travel restrictions to that country.

Ileana is known as a defender of human rights and democracy. She is also active on issues concerning education, children, senior citizens, and women. She has been active in crime victims' issues. She urged that more attention be paid to immigrants' concerns.

Ileana Ros-Lehtinen has never lost an election. In November 2006, she won her ninth term in office. Those who know her say that she is untouchable. Across her district, she is a celebrity.

When she meets the public, she says, "Call my office if I can ever help."

Ileana has achieved many goals because of her hard work. She also knows that people have helped her along the way. "I campaign all year long by talking to people and paying attention to what's going on in my district. I never forget the people that sent me to Washington. When I walk into the Capitol, I still think: 'How did they let a little Cuban refugee like me in here?'"

Remembering the Facts

1. What office did Ileana Ros-Lehtinen win in 1989?

2. Why did the Ros family leave Cuba?

3. How did Ileana's parents give her a strong desire to serve her country?

4. What did Ileana train to be when she was in college?

5. Why were Cuban-American voters upset by the remark, "This is an American (congressional) seat"?

6. What work has Ileana done for the Port of Miami?

7. What has Ileana done for the Everglades?

8. Describe something Ileana has done to oppose communist Cuba.

Understanding the Story

9.   Why do you think Ileana Ros-Lehtinen is such a strong opponent of the Cuban government?

10.   Why is Ileana so popular in her district?

Getting the Main Idea

Why is Ileana Ros-Lehtinen a good role model for the youth of today?

Applying What You've Learned

Make a list of ways a government could put pressure on another country to change its policies.

Jorge Ramos

Journalist

Jorge Ramos has written thousands of news stories. He reads the stories on the television evening news. In over 20 years as a reporter, he has written reports on:

- 60 presidential leaders (of various countries)

- 2 terrorist attacks

- 4 wars

- 2 death threats (to himself)

- 4 political conventions

- 2 assassinations

Jorge has been an evening news anchor since 1986. He works for Univision Spanish-language news. Univision is the fifth largest television network in the United States. In Miami, Los Angeles, and Houston, his news show beats out all the other networks.

The Wall Street Journal has called Jorge Ramos "the star newscaster of Hispanic TV." They named him "Hispanic TV's number one correspondent." The *Journal* went on to say that Jorge is the key to the huge Hispanic voting block. In Hispanic homes across the country, Jorge Ramos is a household name.

Jorge Ramos was born in Mexico City on March 16, 1958. He is the oldest of five children. All the children had blond hair and green eyes. They were all just one year apart in age. Their mother liked to dress them all the same. When the family went out, people noticed them.

As a child, Jorge did not like to study. But he was a quick student and got good grades. His favorite part of school was playing soccer at recess. Jorge was often in trouble with the teachers.

When Jorge was 14, he was chosen to attend the Olympic training camp. He began training as a high jumper. While training, he suffered what he thought was a minor injury to his back. He stopped high jumping and began training hard in the 400-meter for the hurdles. He placed well in the national championships. He hoped to go to the Olympics in 1976.

But the back injury ended Jorge's Olympic dream. He was unable to keep training and was sent home.

Jorge learned something from this time in his life. He found that running helps him handle stress. When a difficult situation comes up, he goes running. He has found that his best ideas come to him while he runs.

Jorge went to the Latin American University in Mexico City. He earned a degree in communication. Jorge worked at a travel agency to pay his tuition. On the job, he learned to type very fast. This skill would come in handy later when writing news reports.

In 1978, Jorge was asked to try out for a job at Televisa. Televisa was the largest telecommunications company in Mexico. When he arrived at Televisa, he found that hundreds of young people were competing for one job.

A few days later, Jorge was hired by Televisa! He would work at XEW radio station in Mexico City. His boss gave him a blank contract to sign. Jorge noticed that the pay was not stated in the contract. His boss told him, "If you want to work, sign here." Jorge signed. The salary turned out to be quite a bit less than he was making at the travel agency. But the job was his opening into the world of journalism.

Jorge's job was to get news stories from all over North America. Not long after he began the job, there was an assassination attempt on President Ronald Reagan. Jorge was the only reporter at the radio station who spoke English and had a passport. He was immediately sent to Washington, DC to cover the story.

Jorge was probably the least experienced foreign correspondent there. He did not know where to go. He didn't know how to get in to the press conferences. He didn't know how to set up an interview. He did complete his assignment, but later said that his efforts left much to be desired.

The trip excited Jorge. He loved the idea of traveling anywhere in the world where news was being made. He also realized that he should make a move from radio to television reporting. Television was where the money was.

Jorge got a job with Televisa's news program, "*Antena Cinco.*" One of his first jobs was to do a story on the eruption of a volcano. He wanted to show that he was a good reporter. So he took his crew as close to the volcano as he could. The ash from the volcano stalled the car's engine. Jorge and the crew had to run! The volcano exploded at the very spot where the car had died. The car was destroyed, but Jorge had his story.

Jorge later said that there was a force more dangerous for his career than the volcano. In Mexico at that time, the government censored the news. This meant that the government told reporters what stories they could write in newspapers or put on news shows. Most reporters did what they were told. But Jorge did not want to work that way. When one of his stories was censored, he quit his job.

Jorge decided he would go to the United States. The problem was how to get out of the country. He had no money. And he knew that if he wanted to work in American television, he could not enter the country illegally. He finally decided that the best thing would be to get accepted to an American college and go on a student visa.

Jorge was accepted to a journalism program at UCLA. He sold his car. Jorge arrived in Los Angeles in 1983. He carried everything he owned in one suitcase. He stayed in a friend's apartment. He bought a television with a hand-sized screen. With this he tried to improve his English.

In 1984, Jorge was hired as a reporter by the local Univision station in Los Angeles. His first job was to cover the 1984 Olympic Games in L.A.

Two years later, Jorge became the host for a morning news program. For the first time, he was a news anchor. Jorge had to learn quickly. He had never read from a teleprompter. He made many mistakes while reading the stories. Jorge was worried he would lose his job. After a while, he realized that none of his bosses got up early enough to see him on the air. He relaxed and worked on getting better at his job.

One morning some executives from the national Spanish language network, Univision, were watching the show. They were looking for someone to do a national morning news show. Jorge was hired and sent to Miami. There he anchored the show "*Mundo Latino.*"

In November 1986, Jorge became the anchor of the evening news. He was only 28. He was one of the youngest anchors in the history of American television.

Jorge wanted to do a newscast that was as good as his American rivals'. He quickly met this goal. In some cities, his newscast had higher ratings than those on NBC, ABC, and CBS.

Jorge still speaks English with a strong Spanish accent. He calls himself "an immigrant," like 30 million other people in the United States. He has not forgotten where he came from. He says that his journey from Mexico to the United States has defined him.

Jorge feels a special responsibility to the Hispanic community. He tries to be a "voice of those who have no voice." He tells stories that other journalists might overlook. He makes sure the world is aware of racism and discrimination against Hispanic Americans.

Jorge has spent much of his career talking about Hispanic issues. He writes a weekly column for more than 40 newspapers in the United States and Latin America. He does a daily radio show that is aired on many stations. Jorge has also written six books.

With all this work, Jorge finds some time for play. Every Saturday, he plays soccer on a Univision team. He says he plays to "try to forget as much as possible the news of the day."

Jorge is married and has two children. He calls his children "new Americans." Both were born in Florida. Jorge, however, has not become an American citizen. Even though he has lived in the United States for more than 20 years, he feels like he belongs to both countries. He says, "I am not from here nor am I from there."

Jorge Ramos says that the "American Dream" is a reality. Anyone who works hard can succeed. He says that this country has given him his children, his career, and his freedom of speech. Jorge Ramos is an immigrant who came to the United States with nothing. He worked hard and achieved his dream.

Remembering the Facts

1. Why was Jorge unable to compete in the Olympics?

2. Why was Jorge willing to work for a low salary at Televisa?

3. What did Jorge discover about himself when he went to Washington, DC to cover the assassination attempt on President Reagan?

4. Why did Jorge leave Mexico?

5. Name one problem Jorge faced when he began his first job as a news anchor.

6. How did Jorge get his job as a national news anchor?

7. What kinds of stories does Jorge include on his newscast?

Understanding the Story

8. Why do you think Jorge calls himself a "voice of those who have no voice"?

9. Why do you think Jorge says he is "not from here nor from there"?

10. How has Jorge achieved the "American Dream"?

Getting the Main Idea

Why do you think Jorge Ramos is a good role model for the youth of today?

Applying What You've Learned

Make a list of issues that you think would be important to Hispanic Americans.

Oscar De La Hoya

Boxer

The barrio of East Los Angeles is not an easy place to grow up. Apartment buildings are run-down. Graffiti covers the walls. There are drug dealers, violence, and guns. In such a place, many young boys join gangs. The gangs give them a place to belong and a sense of safety.

Oscar De La Hoya was born in the barrio of East L.A. He stayed away from gangs. Instead, he went into boxing. He won an Olympic gold medal in 1992. He is the only boxer in history to win world titles in six different weight classes.

Oscar De La Hoya was born on February 4, 1973. His parents had come to Los Angeles from Mexico. Oscar's dad was a professional boxer. But after his three children were born, he got a job as a clerk in an air conditioning business. His mother worked as a seamstress. Although both parents worked hard, there was little money in the family.

By the time Oscar was six, many of his friends had already joined gangs. They wanted Oscar to join too, but he refused. Because he was not part of their group, gang members picked fights with Oscar.

Oscar got tired of losing fights. He went with his father to the neighborhood gym to learn how to box. From the first day, Oscar loved boxing.

Oscar's father let him train at the gym every day. The sport came naturally to Oscar. He won his first fight at the age of seven. He began winning trophies and money. Now the boys in the neighborhood gangs no longer wanted to fight Oscar. He was too good!

When Oscar was eleven years old, he saw another East L.A. fighter on television. Paul Gonzales won the gold medal at the 1984 Olympic Games. Gonzales became a hero for Oscar and for many others in the barrio.

From that point on, Oscar De La Hoya knew exactly what he wanted to do with his life. He began working with a trainer, Robert Alcazar. He followed his dream with great focus. It wasn't long before Oscar discovered his strongest point. It was his powerful left hand.

Oscar trained using what he calls his "D formula." His three D's are dedication, discipline, and desire. The D formula worked for him! At age 15, Oscar became the Junior Olympic champion in the 119-pound weight class. The next year, he won the national Golden Gloves title in the 125-pound class.

In 1990, at age 17, Oscar De La Hoya won the U.S. Amateur Boxing Championship. Also that year, he won the gold medal at the Goodwill Games in Seattle. Both of these wins were in the 125-pound class. During his amateur career, Oscar fought 228 matches and lost only 5!

Oscar kept up with his schoolwork, as well. He was a student at Garfield High School. This tough school was made famous in the movie *Stand and Deliver*, starring Edward James Olmos. When he was on the road on the boxing circuit, Oscar had a tutor to help him with his assignments. He graduated right on schedule in June 1991.

In the meantime, Oscar's mother had been ill with cancer. She died at the age of 38. Cecilia De La Hoya had been Oscar's biggest fan. Just before she died, she told Oscar that her dream for him was to win an Olympic gold medal.

In 1992, two years after his mother died, Oscar went to the Olympic Games in Barcelona, Spain. He had trained hard and made the U.S. Olympic team in the 132-pound weight class.

In the gold medal round, Oscar fought one of the few boxers who had beaten him before. Later, he said that he had felt his mother's presence as if she were sitting at the side of the ring. This gave him the confidence he needed to win.

Oscar won the fight. In fact, he was the only U.S. boxer to win a gold medal at the Olympics that year. He was proud and happy. He danced around the ring holding a U.S. flag in one hand and a Mexican flag in the other. But the first thing he did after returning home was to go to the cemetery and lay his medal on his mother's grave. "She was my inspiration," he said.

Just three months after the Olympics, Oscar turned pro. He kept winning his professional fights until he had a 21–0 record.

Finally, he came to what he thought of as his real test. He would fight the World Boxing Council Champion, Julio Cesar Chavez. Chavez was ten years older than Oscar De La Hoya. He was Mexico's most popular boxer, having won 97 out of 99 fights. Oscar knew that this fight would be his most difficult ever.

Oscar trained hard. He ran six miles a day. He did at least 140 push-ups to build upper-body strength. Finally, he was ready. The fight did not last long. In fact, it was very one-sided. The referee stopped the match two minutes into the fourth round. He needed to protect Julio Chavez from serious injury. Now Oscar De La Hoya was the new World Boxing Council Super-Lightweight Champion!

Oscar De La Hoya continued his winning streak. In 1997, he won all five fights he entered. He made the most money a non-heavyweight fighter has ever made. *Forbes* magazine listed his 1997 winnings as $37 million. Oscar De La Hoya had become the "Golden Boy" of boxing.

In 2002, Oscar fought Fernando Vargas. He won the fight in the eleventh round. In 2003, he kept his WBC and WBA World Junior Middleweight Championships by beating Yori Boy Campas.

In 2004, Oscar challenged Felix Sturm for the WBO World Middleweight title. He won the fight. This made him the first boxer in history to win world titles in six different weight classes! He has won world crowns at 130 to 160 pounds.

In 2006, Oscar won a fight against Ricardo Mayorga. He said he would not fight again in 2006. He plans retire after 2007.

Oscar has been busy outside the boxing ring, too. He has promoted (organized) fights. He has his own company: Golden Boy Promotions. He has hosted television shows.

Oscar has another talent. He has always loved to sing. In 2000, he recorded an album of Latin pop music called *Oscar*. A single from the album *Ven a Mi* was nominated for a Grammy award.

In 2001, he married Millie Corretjer. She is a pop singer from Puerto Rico. The couple has one child.

Oscar has moved out of the barrio, but he hasn't forgotten his roots. In his wallet, he carries a food stamp to remind him of leaner days. He started the Oscar De La Hoya Foundation to help needy children.

Oscar De La Hoya once said, "My favorite thing about being a champion is that I can be a role model for kids." He has done this in many ways.

In 1996, Oscar paid $500,000 for the run-down gym where he used to train as a boy. He spent another $250,000 to remodel it. Now the gym is known as the Oscar De La Hoya Youth Boxing Center. Oscar hopes it will be a safe haven for kids who want to escape the street gangs as he did.

Oscar has given money to Garfield High students for scholarships. He has also donated money to the school for activities.

He tries to set a good example in the way he acts, too. Some fighters use bad language and brag when they win a fight. But Oscar De La Hoya says his mother raised him to have good manners. He speaks quietly and is respectful of other fighters.

Oscar's pleasant personality and good looks have made him one of the most likeable athletes in the world. He has given boxing a new image. He is truly boxing's "Golden Boy." He is one of boxing's all-time greats.

Remembering the Facts

1. Why did Oscar De La Hoya begin learning to box at age six?

2. Explain Oscar's "D formula."

3. How did Oscar keep up in school when he traveled?

4. What was Mrs. De La Hoya's dream for her son?

5. What title did Oscar win by beating Julio Cesar Chavez?

6. Why does Oscar carry a food stamp in his wallet?

7. Name two ways Oscar has helped the youth of his old neighborhood.

8. What "first" did Oscar achieve in 2004?

Understanding the Story

9. Why do you think joining a gang is appealing to youth living in the barrio?

10. Why do you think Oscar plans to retire at age 34?

Getting the Main Idea

How do you think Oscar is a good role model for American youth?

Applying What You've Learned

Write a paragraph in which you name your favorite sport and explain why it is your favorite.

Vocabulary

Cesar Chavez

La Causa	pesticides	boycott	nonviolent protest
union	civil rights	huelga	migrant workers
strike	register		

Dolores Huerta

illegal	negotiator	amnesty
immigrant	pension	organizer
lobbyist	pesticide	

Joan Baez

Quakers	debut	soprano
folk music	drafted	human rights
nonviolence	dyslexic	octave

Ellen Ochoa

space shuttle	scholarship	ozone layer
patent	ultraviolet rays	atmosphere
NASA		

Jaime Escalente

mediocre	graffiti	determination
discipline	calculus	Advanced Placement
barrio		

Edward James Olmos

immigrant	convicted	narrator
drama	prejudice	mannerisms
nominated	poverty	

Judy Baca

mural	prehistoric	Depression
public art	rival	ethnic minorities

Sandra Cisneros

literature	publication	literary agent	vintage

Roberto Clemente

foreman	league	career
charity	relief effort	survivors
championship	fielding	Baseball Hall of Fame

Henry B. Gonzalez

Representative	bribe	army intelligence
restricted	fraud	racial segregation
assassin	violate	assassination
politics	senate	translation
crisis	filibuster	

Roberto Goizueta

communist	slogan	international	Caribbean

Antonia Novello

surgeon general	immunization	alcohol
resident	surgery	intern
confirmed	public health	pediatrician

José Feliciano

ghetto	national anthem	recording artist	gold record
mandolin	accordion	symphony	
coffeehouse	timbales	bongos	

Ileana Ros-Lehtinen

exile	opponent	election	dredge
district	overthrow	democracy	

Jorge Ramos

journalist	assassination	teleprompter
anchor	correspondent	immigrant
network	censored	visa

Oscar De La Hoya

barrio	Olympics	inspiration
graffiti	dedication	seamstress
discipline	amateur	circuit

Answer Key

Cesar Chavez

Remembering the Facts

1. They could not pay the taxes.
2. It is work that requires bending over all day to pick crops.
3. They felt powerless. They didn't speak English, and many were not citizens. The growers were rich and powerful. Workers who angered them might lose their jobs and get sent back to Mexico.
4. He read a lot.
5. The CSO worked to help Mexican Americans better themselves.
6. He used his life savings of $1,200.
7. marches, boycotts, fasts

Understanding the Story

8. People on both sides would have been killed. The farm workers would have been feared and would not have gained the sympathy of the American public.
9. Both fought for civil rights. Both continued the fight at risk of personal danger. Both made impressive gains for oppressed minorities.
10. His passion was for his work. Money did not matter to him.

Getting the Main Idea

His is an inspiring story of how one person can make a huge difference in spite of overwhelming odds.

Applying What You've Learned

Answers will vary. Students should mention long hours, low pay, poor living conditions, and lack of adequate food.

Dolores Huerta

Remembering the Facts

1. She modeled strength, independence, and ambition. She helped those who were less fortunate.
2. He went back to school and earned a degree. He was elected to the New Mexico state legislature and worked for better labor laws.
3. She thought she could be more effective addressing the roots of the problem.
4. the strike against the California grape growers
5. It was the first law of its kind in the United States. It guaranteed farm workers the right to unionize, and required growers to negotiate with the union.
6. Workers became ill or died from contact with pesticides. Their children suffered birth defects.
7. It works to organize poor communities to get gains for themselves.

Understanding the Story

8. She won for farm workers the first medical and pension plans, the first credit union, higher wages, better housing, safer working conditions, and the right to unionize.
9. King worked to gain civil rights for blacks. Huerta worked to gain basic rights for farm workers.
10. Today, immigrants are still vulnerable. Many are still poor and are treated unfairly. Those who are in the country illegally have no rights. There is much work to be done to solve this problem.

Getting the Main Idea

Dolores Huerta dedicated her life to making life better for a group of people who were poor and uneducated. She showed great courage and selflessness as she defended the rights of others. She worked all her life to help those in need.

Applying What You've Learned

Answers will vary.

Joan Baez

Remembering the Facts

1. nonviolence
2. She was dyslexic.
3. folk music
4. Newport Jazz Festival in 1959
5. Any two of the following: civil rights movement; antiwar movement; Cesar Chavez and the farm workers

6. to improve human rights around the world

7. Live Aid, Amnesty International's Conspiracy of Hope, People's Summit, etc.

8. the United States' invasion of Iraq

Understanding the Story

9. Her message of peace is still important for the world to hear.

10. Music and the arts give us hope and beauty even in the worst of times. They refresh our souls and remind us of the good parts of life.

Getting the Main Idea

She is a good role model because she has devoted her life to causes and principles she believes in.

Applying What You've Learned

It makes them think about important issues. Her songs give inspiration and healing.

Ellen Ochoa

Remembering the Facts

1. Her mother stressed the value of education and hard work.

2. She wanted to stay close to home to help her mother with her two younger brothers.

3. the flute

4. She had become interested in being an astronaut and wanted to learn more about flying.

5. optical processing

6. the earth's atmosphere; changes taking place in the ozone layer; the earth's climate changes

7. It protects the earth from the sun and its harmful ultraviolet rays.

8. Anyone can succeed if he or she works hard enough in school and on the job.

Understanding the Story

9. Ellen's mother practiced what she preached. She taught her children that education was important. They could see how hard she worked to get an education.

10. She feels that her fame has put her in a position to have some influence. Women are underrepresented in math and science. They may not have the confidence to try; she hopes to encourage them.

Getting the Main Idea

Ellen Ochoa is a good role model because she achieved her success through hard work, both in school and on the job.

Applying What You've Learned

Answers will vary.

Jaime Escalente

Remembering the Facts

1. math and science

2. Teachers in Bolivia were so poorly paid that he had to work three or four jobs.

3. He had to repeat five years of college at an American college.

4. Any three of the following: In the barrio, most students came from poor Hispanic families; gangs; graffiti; trash all over school grounds; most students dropped out; little interest in education

5. to get college credit for a course taken in high school

6. because so many from one school passed the test; because many students worked one of the questions the same way

7. *Stand and Deliver*

8. Determination + Hard Work + Discipline

Understanding the Story

9. To achieve success, you must first make up your mind that you want to succeed (determination). You must then work hard and be disciplined to keep at it.

10. To be successful and feel good about yourself, it is important to be really good at something. Doing an inadequate job will not allow you to succeed.

Getting the Main Idea

Escalente is an example of a person who persevered in the face of great odds to do something he loved. He believed that underprivileged students could achieve, and he set out to prove it to them.

Applying What You've Learned

Answers will vary.

Edward James Olmos

Remembering the Facts

1. by becoming a baseball star

2. to overcome his fear of public speaking

3. a group of young Mexican-Americans wrongly convicted of murder in L.A. in 1942

4. *Miami Vice*

5. *Stand and Deliver*

6. He uses himself as an example.

7. appeared on TV, talked to people, helped clean up

8. Any two of the following: prisons, detention centers, Indian reservations, teachers' meetings

Understanding the Story

9. He practices what he preaches. He lived in a poor area of Los Angeles and worked his way up. He sets a good example and relates well to students.

10. He portrays Hispanics accurately in his work. He does not do stereotyped roles. He helps Hispanic youth see that they can better themselves.

Getting the Main Idea

Olmos is a role model not only because is he a fine actor, but also because he spends much of his time doing public service work, mostly with youth who might be prone to a life of crime and violence.

Applying What You've Learned

Answers will vary. Explain why nonviolence works best in the long run, and that the lives and property of innocent people are being destroyed. Explain that violence will not undo the wrong that was previously done. Ask respected leaders in the community to speak to the people, as well.

Judy Baca

Remembering the Facts

1. *The Great Wall of Los Angeles*

2. the history of California

3. Murals are an old Mexican art form. She used the kids' love of graffiti to interest them in doing murals.

4. She was active in antiwar protests during the Vietnam War.

5. Any three of the following: prehistoric animals roaming along the tar pits; Cabrillo arriving by ship; Mexicans and Yankees fighting over gold; Chinese workers building the railroad; migrant farm workers working; hungry people lining up for food during the Depression; Japanese Americans being interned during World War II; freedom riders working for civil rights

6. It took place over five summers with the help of 200 kids. Baca organized the project and raised money for it. She hired other workers and kids to join in.

7. Baca painted seven panels. The mural was sent to other countries where artists added more panels.

8. repairing *The Great Wall*

Understanding the Story

9. Answers will vary. She ended up teaching art to a large number of kids. She also motivated kids from a wide variety of backgrounds to forget their differences and work together.

10. She meant that when people view artwork, they are exposed to the ideas the artist wants to portray. If you see a painting, you are aware of the idea the artist wants to convey. Similarly, if you hear a piece of music, it influences your thinking. You may not even be aware of how it has changed your thinking or your mood at the time.

Getting the Main Idea

Judy Baca is a good role model because she is living what she believes. From a young age, she wanted to work for peace and to solve social problems. Her "public art" has influenced many young people to forget gangs and fighting, and work together in peace. She has brought them pride in their history. Now, with the *World Wall*, she is hoping to spread her ideas around the world.

Applying What You've Learned

Murals will vary.

Sandra Cisneros

Remembering the Facts

1. Her father would get homesick for Mexico.

2. She was shy. Reading became an escape from loneliness.

3. She spent a lot of time observing people.

4. She realized her experiences were different from everyone else's. She accepted herself and went on to tell her story.

5. *The House on Mango Street*

6. She talks about the lives of the people living on Mango Street, a poor Hispanic community in Chicago.

7. Her childhood will always be a part of who she is.

Understanding the Story

8. People who read a lot gain a sense of language and style. They learn how to put thoughts together to tell a story. They gain a rich background of ideas and thoughts.

9. Hispanic-American culture is part of the fabric of America. *The House on Mango Street* shows that culture and lifestyle.

10. The experiences you have growing up are an integral part of your being. You can never completely leave them behind.

Getting the Main Idea

Sandra Cisneros is a good role model because she learned to accept herself as she is and to celebrate that in her work. She has dedicated herself to telling the story of her people, her race, and her gender.

Applying What You've Learned

Answers will vary.

Roberto Clemente

Remembering the Facts

1. The Santurce Crabbers

2. because he had given them his word

3. He felt like an outsider. He faced racial discrimination, and different food and customs. He did not speak English well.

4. swinging a light bat; a car accident

5. the Pittsburgh Pirates

6. He went to Puerto Rico and worked with kids.

7. to make sure they got to those who needed help

8. Any three of the following: 4 National League batting championships; National League's Most Valuable Player 1966, 1971; 12 Golden Glove awards; Baseball Hall of Fame

Understanding the Story

9. He was a local boy who had made it big in the States. He had won fame and fortune, but he was never too busy to help those in need. He devoted much energy to working with children in Puerto Rico.

10. He felt a responsibility to help humankind. But he did not want praise or recognition for doing what was right. He felt his purpose in life was to help others who needed him.

Getting the Main Idea

Roberto Clemente was a National League superstar who centered his life around helping those less fortunate. He is an excellent role model on how to live your life.

Applying What You've Learned

Answers will vary.

Henry B. Gonzalez

Remembering the Facts

1. U.S. Congressman

2. He didn't know any English. He was one of just a few Mexican Americans in his class.

3. Any two of the following: minority rights; better housing; prevention of a sales tax

4. by taking part in a 36-hour filibuster

5. John F. Kennedy

6. The Affordable Housing Act

7. the savings and loan crisis

8. a reputation for honesty and independence

Understanding the Story

9. He fought for the rights of minorities. He fought for better housing. He fought hard for the rights of his citizens.

10. Gonzalez had a reputation for honesty. He could not be bought or bribed. He did not get involved in "dirty politics." He fought for whatever he thought was right, even if it was not popular.

Getting the Main Idea

Gonzalez overcame the racial prejudice of the 1950s by working hard to win respect. He fought hard for his beliefs.

Applying What You've Learned

Answers will vary. Immigration, housing for minorities, etc.

Roberto Goizueta

Remembering the Facts

1. The country became communist. Fidel Castro was taking over businesses and properties. Many people were jailed.
2. Woodruff became Goizueta's mentor, and appointed him CEO of the company.
3. Chairman and Chief Executive Officer (CEO) of Coca-Cola
4. There were older, more experienced people in line. He was from Cuba.
5. trying to change the formula of Coke® (New Coke)
6. There were two Cokes. The old Coke was called Coca-Cola Classic. The new Coke continued to be sold.
7. the Olympic Games
8. Atlanta, Georgia

Understanding the Story

9. He worked hard and was interested in everything.
10. Coke had become a part of the American way of life. It was part of American culture and identity. People wanted it to stay the same.

Getting the Main Idea

Goizueta is an example of how anyone can get ahead with hard work and determination.

Applying What You've Learned

Students should choose a slogan and create an ad for Coke.

Antonia Novello

Remembering the Facts

1. She was the first woman, first Hispanic, and first Puerto Rican to be surgeon general.
2. She had a birth defect and was often ill as a child. Her doctors were her heroes.
3. She felt that she could make more of a contribution working for the government.
4. to protect and improve the health of the American people
5. AIDS, childhood immunizations, teenage drinking and smoking, etc.
6. She felt that the ads showed drinking to be fun and necessary to have a good life. She thought that the cartoon characters were used to appeal to the very young.
7. It gave her a chance to improve children's health around the world.

Understanding the Story

8. She believed that young people are our future. By discouraging young people from using alcohol or tobacco, they will live healthier lives.
9. She did not think it was a realistic goal.
10. Eliminating ads that appealed to kids was a way to prevent some teens from starting to smoke. She knew tobacco was a major preventable cause of disease.

Getting the Main Idea

Novello has dedicated her life to the service of others, especially those who cannot speak up for themselves. She has worked hard to make a difference in the lives of the young, minority groups, and the poor in the United States.

Applying What You've Learned

Some advertising techniques students might use include: using a cartoon character such as "Joe Camel;" making smokers look strong and independent; and portraying smokers or drinkers as having more fun, having more girlfriends or boyfriends, and getting more out of life in general.

José Feliciano

Remembering the Facts

1. blindness, poverty
2. He tricked the managers into listening to him play.
3. An RCA Records executive came to hear another musician and heard Feliciano play.
4. Latin America (Central and South America)
5. "Light My Fire"
6. the guitar
7. hard work
8. "the happy one"

Understanding the Story

9. Many people felt it was unpatriotic to sing the national anthem in a "Spanish soul" style. They felt it should be done in only one way: the traditional version.

10. Since he was blind, he concentrated solely on his music with a dedication unusual for a small child, spending most of his free time practicing. If he had had his sight, it is likely that he would not have developed his talent to such a degree so early.

Getting the Main Idea

Feliciano is a good role model because he is a hard worker. He puts everything he's got into what he is doing. He says that hard work is the magic ingredient in success in any field.

Applying What You've Learned

Students could mention his awards, his hit records, the date and place of the concert, the cost for tickets, etc.

Ileana Ros-Lehtinen

Remembering the Facts

1. She was elected to the United States Congress.

2. Castro came to power.

3. They decided to raise their children as loyal Americans.

4. a teacher, a principal

5. It implied to them that they were not "real" Americans.

6. cleaning and dredging the Miami River and Port of Miami so big ships can enter

7. cleaning up the water

8. against human rights violations; penalties for companies that trade with Cuba

Understanding the Story

9. When Castro took over the country, her family was forced to flee, leaving behind their home and possessions. She feels that he has destroyed her native land.

10. She works for their concerns.

Getting the Main Idea

She is a good role model because she has worked hard to achieve her goals. She is working hard for all the people of her congressional district.

Applying What You've Learned

Answers will vary. Students could mention boycotts, trade sanctions, refusing to allow the country into international organizations, etc.

Jorge Ramos

Remembering the Facts

1. because of a back injury

2. He knew it was his opening into journalism.

3. He thought it was exciting to travel to wherever news was being made.

4. One of his stories was censored.

5. He couldn't read from the teleprompter. He made many mistakes while reading.

6. Executives from the national Spanish network saw his show and offered him a job.

7. He makes sure to include stories that affect Hispanic Americans. He tells stories of racism and discrimination.

Understanding the Story

8. Many Hispanic Americans are poor and have no power. He makes sure that their stories are not lost.

9. He feels torn between the country of his birth and the United States where he has lived for 20 years.

10. He came to the United States with no money. He worked hard and achieved success.

Getting the Main Idea

He worked hard to achieve his dream. He acted upon his principles by leaving Mexico when his story was censored. He was not discouraged but kept working until he met his goals.

Applying What You've Learned

Answers will vary. Students might mention the following:

- U.S./Mexican border issues
- illegal immigrants in the United States
- treatment of migrant farm workers
- attempts to make English the official language of the United States
- bilingual education in the public schools, etc.

Oscar De La Hoya

Remembering the Facts

1. Other kids were picking on him because he refused to join a gang.

2. The three D's were determination, desire, and discipline. To win you have to be determined that you will win. You must really desire to win. And you must be disciplined to stick to your training.

3. He had a tutor.

4. She wanted him to win an Olympic gold medal.

5. WBC (World Boxing Council) Super-Lightweight Champion

6. It reminds him of the days when he was poor.

7. Any two of the following: renovated a gym for local youth, donated money to Garfield students for scholarships, donated money to the school for activities

8. He became the first boxer to win world titles in six weight classes.

Understanding the Story

9. It provides protection (safety in numbers). It gives them something to belong to.

10. He remembers that his father retired when he had children. He wants to retire while he is at the top of his skills, not after he starts going downhill.

Getting the Main Idea

He is a good role model because he set goals for himself and works hard to make them happen. Now that he has achieved his goals, he works to help others who are less fortunate.

Applying What You've Learned

Answers will vary.

Additional Activities

Cesar Chavez

1. Read John Steinbeck's book *The Grapes of Wrath*. This is a vivid account of the life of migrant workers in the 1930s in California.

2. Mahatma Gandhi was Chavez's hero. Read more about Gandhi's philosophy.

3. Read more about the Great Depression of the 1930s. Why did so many small farmers lose their farms at this time, as Chavez's parents did?

4. Use the Internet to learn about the goals and activities of the United Farm Workers today.

Dolores Huerta

1. Use the Internet to read more about the jobs done by migrant farm workers.

2. In small groups, discuss the issue of illegal immigrants. Brainstorm a list of ways to solve this problem. Present your ideas to the class.

3. Use the Internet to find out what issues the UFW is tackling today.

Joan Baez

1. Read Baez's autobiography *And a Voice to Sing With*.

2. Listen to some of Baez's CDs. What themes do you hear running through her music?

Ellen Ochoa

1. Franklin Chang-Diaz was the first male Hispanic astronaut. Use the Internet to find out more about his life.

2. Use the Internet to find out about the space shuttle program today.

3. Find out more about the ozone layer. Learn why scientists are concerned about the fact that it is thinning.

Jaime Escalente

1. Watch the movie *Stand and Deliver*, starring Edward James Olmos as Jaime Escalente.

2. Find out what types of Advanced Placement courses are available in your local high school.

3. Choose a teacher that you admire. Write a paragraph explaining how that teacher inspires students to succeed.

Edward James Olmos

1. Watch one of Edward James Olmos' movies. Give a summary about it in class.

2. Watch an episode of *Battlestar Gallactica*. Give a description of Olmos' character to the class.

Judy Baca

1. Use the Internet to find out more about one of these famous Mexican mural painters: Diego Rivera, David Alfaro Siqueiros, or José Clemente Orozco.

2. Make a mural of your life. Divide a sheet of paper into six sections. In each section, draw a picture showing something important in your life.

Sandra Cisneros

1. Write a story or poem about your childhood. Include things that would make you different from other people.

2. Read the book *The House on Mango Street.* Read a selection from one of Cisneros' other books.

3. Read Cisneros' newest book, *Caramelo.*

4. Visit Cisneros' web site at www.sandracisneros.com.

Roberto Clemente

1. Read and report on another Hispanic-American baseball player of your choice. Some examples are: Luis Aparicio, Rod Carew, Orlando Cepeda, Martin Dihigo, Tony Fernandez, Lefty Gomez, Keith Hernandez, Al Lopez, Juan Marichal, José Mendez, Orestes Minoso, Tony Oliva, Alejandro Oms, Luis Tiant, Fernando Valenzuela, Pedro Guerroro, Rafael Santana, George Bell, Joaquin Andujar, Alfredo Griffin, Julio Franco, Ozzie Virgil, Felipe Alou, Mario Soto, Sammy Sosa, and many more.

2. Find Puerto Rico on a map and research its history.

3. Use the Internet to read about the earthquake in Nicaragua in 1972.

4. Use the Internet to read about Branch Rickey, who was the manager of the Pittsburg Pirates for part of Clemente's career. Branch Rickey was the man who signed Jackie Robinson, the first African American in professional baseball.

5. Use the Internet to read about the old Negro League baseball teams.

Henry B. Gonzalez

1. Read more about the assassination of President John F. Kennedy and the conspiracy theory favored by Gonzalez.

2. Read more about the savings and loan scandal.

3. Draw a political cartoon showing Henry B. Gonzalez fighting for one of his many causes. Or make up a current example using a cause you think Gonzalez would fight for.

Roberto Goizueta

1. Use the Internet to read about the story of the Coca-Cola Company.

2. Imagine you are a newspaper writer. Write a short newspaper article telling why the Coke formula should not be changed. Write a catchy headline to go with the story.

3. Use the Internet to find out more about Fidel Castro and his rise to power in Cuba.

4. Find out the price of a share of Coca-Cola stock today. Use the Internet or look in the newspaper.

Antonia Novello

1. Make a collage of ads for alcohol and tobacco companies. You might cut ads out of newspapers or magazines. Or write a summary describing ads you have seen. For each ad in your collection, explain how the ad tries to make smoking or drinking look appealing.

2. Report on one of the following problems: alcohol use among teens, teen smoking, AIDS among teens, childhood immunizations.

3. Discuss immunizations that are required for a child to attend public school. What are these immunizations for? Why do some children not receive these immunizations?

4. Use the Internet to learn more about UNICEF, the United Nations Children's Fund. This group works for children's health and rights. Visit their web site at www.unicef.org.

José Feliciano

1. Listen to one of José Feliciano's albums. Discuss his style.

2. Design a cover for a CD of one of José's songs.

3. Find José's birthplace, Lares, Puerto Rico, on a map. Read more about that part of Puerto Rico.

4. Use the Internet to read about "Spanish Harlem," the Hispanic ghetto in New York City.

Ileana Ros-Lehtinen

1. Use the Internet to learn more about Fidel Castro and his rise to power in Cuba. Find out why so many middle- and upper-class Cubans fled to the United States in 1960.

2. Find out more about the city of Miami and its Cuban-American population.

3. Visit Ros-Lehtinen's web site at www.house.gov/ros-lehtinen/ to learn more about her activities today.

Jorge Ramos

1. Have a class debate on a current topic affecting Hispanic Americans. Examples:
    - U.S./Mexican border issues
    - illegal immigrants in the United States
    - treatment of migrant farm workers
    - attempts to make English the official language of the United States
    - bilingual education in the public schools

2. Make a poster illustrating Hispanic foods. Label their origins (Cuban, Mexican, or Puerto Rican).

3. Watch a Spanish language news show. Write a paragraph comparing it to a news show done in English.

Oscar De La Hoya

1. Use the Internet to find out about another famous boxer. Examples are Muhammad Ali and Sugar Ray Leonard.

2. Research the rules and scoring procedure for a WBC boxing match.

3. Find out what Oscar De La Hoya is doing now.

References

General References

Benson, Sonia G., editor. *The Hispanic American Almanac, third edition.* Farmington Hills, MI: The Gale Group, 2003.

Catalano, Julie. *The Mexican Americans.* New York: Chelsea House Publishers, 1996.

Contemporary Hispanic Biography. *Farmington Hills, MI: Gale Group, 2002.*

Dwyer, Christopher. *The Dominican Americans.* New York: Chelsea House Publishers, 1991.

Gernand, Renee. *The Cuban Americans.* New York: Chelsea House Publishers, 1995.

Palmisano, Joseph, ed. *Notable Hispanic American Women: Book II.* Farmington Hills, MI: Thomson Gale, 2003.

Telgen, Diane, and Kamp, Jim, eds. *Notable Hispanic-American Women.* Detroit: Gale Research, 1993.

Cesar Chavez

"Cesar Chavez." *Current Biography Yearbook.* New York: H. W. Wilson Co., 1969, pp. 86–89.

"Cesar Chavez." *Current Biography Yearbook.* New York: H. W. Wilson Co., 1993, Obituaries.

Geiger, Kimberly. "State to establish a Hall of Fame." *San Francisco Chronicle:* 8/01/2006.

Krull, Kathleen. *Harvesting Hope: The Story of Cesar Chavez.* New York: Harcourt Childrens' Books, 2003.

Roberts, Naurice. *Cesar Chavez and La Causa.* Chicago: Children's Press, 1986.

Dolores Huerta

"Dolores Huerta." *Current Biography Yearbook 1997.* New York: H. W. Wilson Co., pp. 234–237.

"Dolores Huerta." www.gale.com/free_resources.htm. 2006 Thomson Gale.

Dolores Huerta Foundation Biography. www.doloreshuerta.org.

Schiff, Karenna Gore. *Lighting the Way: Nine Women Who Changed Modern America.* New York: Hyperion, 2005, pp. 297–340.

Joan Baez

Baez, Joan. *And a Voice to Sing With: A Memoir.* New York: Summit Books, 1987.

Hajdu, David. *Positively 4th Street: The Lives and Times of Joan Baez, Bob Dylan, Mimi Baez Farina and Richard Farina.* New York: Farrar, Straus, and Giroux, 2001.

Official web site of Joan Baez: www.joanbaez.com.

Telgen, Diane, and Kamp, Jim, eds. *Notable Hispanic-American Women.* Detroit: Gale Research, 1993, pp. 42–45.

Ellen Ochoa

"Ellen Ochoa." *Contemporary Hispanic Biography Vol 1.* Farmington Hills, MI: Gale Group, 2002.

"Ellen Ochoa." NASA web site: www.jsc.nasa.gov/Bios/htmlbios/ochoa.html.

"Ellen Ochoa." www.gale.com.

Iverson, Teresa. *Ellen Ochoa.* New Hampshire: Raintree, 2005.

Telgen, Diane, and Kamp, Jim, eds. *Notable Hispanic-American Women.* Detroit: Gale Research, 1993, pp. 296–299.

Jaime Escalente

Benson, Sonia G., editor. *The Hispanic American Almanac, Vol. 3.* Farmington Hills, MI: The Gale Group, 2003, pp. 694–5.

Mathews, Jay. "Escalente Still Stands and Delivers." *Time,* July 20, 1992.

———. *Escalente: The Best Teacher in America.* New York: Holt, 1988.

Warner Brothers. *Stand and Deliver* (film). 1988.

Edward James Olmos

Benson, Sonia G., editor. *The Hispanic American Almanac, third ed.* Farmington Hills, MI: The Gale Group, 2003, pp. 760–761.

Current Biography Yearbook. New York: H. W. Wilson Co., 1992, pp. 426–430.

"Edward James Olmos." www.gale.com/free_resources.

Garcia, Guy D. "Burning With Passion." *Time,* July 13, 1988.

Johnson, Steven. *Walk, Don't Run.* Wilkes-Barrie, PA: Kallisti Publishing, 2005.

Szegedy-Maszak, Marianne. "The Activist Actor." *USA Weekend,* May 20–22, 1994.

Judy Baca

Bloom, Bernard. *Art for the People.* Farmington Hills, MI: Thomson Gale, 2005.

"Judith F. Baca." *Contemporary Hispanic Biography Vol. 2.* Farmington Hills, MI: Gale Group, 2002.

"Judith Francisca Baca." *The Hispanic-American Almanac, Third Edition.* Farmington Hills, MI: The Gale Group, 2003, pp. 652–653.

Lippard, Lucy R. *Mixed Blessings: New Art in a Multicultural America.* New York: Pantheon Books, 1990, pp. 170–171.

Telgen, Diane, and Kamp, Jim, eds. *Notable Hispanic-American Women.* Detroit: Gale Research, 1993, pp. 35–38.

Henry B. Gonzalez

Benson, Sonia G., editor. *The Hispanic American Almanac, Third Edition.* Farmington Hills, MI: The Gale Group, 2003. pp. 712–713.

"Henry B. Gonzalez." Current Biography Yearbook. New York: H. W. Wilson Co., 1993, pp. 214–217.

Newlon, Clarke. *Famous Mexican Americans.* New York: Dodd, Mead, 1972.

Roberto Goizueta

Benson, Sonia G., editor. "Roberto Goizeuta." *The Hispanic American Almanac, Third Edition.* 2003, Farmington Hills, MI: The Gale Group, 2003, pp. 166–169.

Grossman, Laurie M. "Coke's Move to Retain Goizueta Spotlights a Succession Problem." *The Wall Street Journal,* May 13, 1994.

Huey, John. "The World's Best Brand." *Fortune,* May 31, 1993.

Ingham, John N., and Feldman, Lynne B., eds. *Contemporary American Business Leaders: A Biographical Dictionary.* Westport, CT: Greenwood Press, 1990, pp. 166–176.

"Roberto Goizueta." *Current Biography Yearbook 1996.* New York: H.T. Wilson Co. pp. 166–167.

Antonia Novello

"Antonia Novello." Current Biography Yearbook. New York: H. W. Wilson Co., 1992, pp. 422–426.

Stille, Darlene. *Extraordinary Women of Medicine.* New York: Children's Press, 1997, pp. 261–264.

José Feliciano

Clifford, Mike, ed. *The Harmony Illustrated History of Rock.* New York: Harmony Books, 1986, p. 80.

Official web site: www.josefeliciano.com.

Pareles, Jon, and Romanowski, Patricia, eds. *The Rolling Stone Encyclopedia of Rock and Roll.* New York: Rolling Stone Press, 1983, pp. 184–187.

Rostova, Carolina Ruiz. "A Latin Legend in the Jazz World." *Stamford Advocate,* January 7, 1994.

Jorge Ramos

"Jorge Ramos." Hispanic Magazine.com. www.hispaniconline.com/magazine/2001/jan_feb/CoverStory/.

"Jorge Ramos, a biography." www.jorgeramos.com/eng_bio.htm.

Ramos, Jorge. *No Borders: A Journalist's Search for Home.* New York: HarperCollins Publishers, 2002.

Ileana Ros-Lehtinen

Black, Chris. "Exile Politics Shaped Passions of New Florida Congresswoman." *Boston Globe*, August 31, 1989.

"Ileana Ros-Lehtinen." *Current Biography Yearbook 2000. New York: H.T. Wilson Co.,* pp. 474–5.

Official web site: www.house.gov/ros-lehtinen/biography.html.

Telgen, Diane, and Kamp, Jim, eds. *Notable Hispanic-American Women.* Detroit: Gale Research, 1991, pp. 356–358.

Oscar De La Hoya

"Hit List/Oscar De La Hoya." *The Wall Street Journal,* September 23, 2006.

"Oscar De La Hoya." *Current Biography, Vol. 58 No. 1.* New York: H. T. Wilson Co., January, 1997.

"Oscar De La Hoya." www.latinosportslegends.com.

"Oscar De La Hoya." http://en.wikipedia.org.

Share Your Bright Ideas

We want to hear from you!

Your name_____Date_____

School name_____

School address_____

City _____State _____Zip_____Phone number (_____)_____

Grade level(s) taught_____Subject area(s) taught_____

Where did you purchase this publication?_____

In what month do you purchase a majority of your supplements?_____

What moneys were used to purchase this product?

____School supplemental budget   ____Federal/state funding   ____Personal

Please "grade" this Walch publication in the following areas:

Quality of service you received when purchasing .... A   B   C   D
Ease of use.. A   B   C   D
Quality of content... A   B   C   D
Page layout .... A   B   C   D
Organization of material .... A   B   C   D
Suitability for grade level .... A   B   C   D
Instructional value... A   B   C   D

COMMENTS:_____

_____

What specific supplemental materials would help you meet your current—or future—instructional needs?

_____

Have you used other Walch publications? If so, which ones?_____

May we use your comments in upcoming communications?   ____Yes   ____No

Please **FAX** this completed form to **888-991-5755**, or mail it to

Customer Service, Walch Publishing, P. O. Box 658, Portland, ME 04104-0658

We will send you a **FREE GIFT** in appreciation of your feedback. **THANK YOU!**